THE
BANALITY
OF
SUICIDE
TERRORISM

RELATED TITLES FROM POTOMAC BOOKS

The Path to Paradise:
The Inner World of Suicide Bombers and Their Dispatchers
—Anat Berko

Triumph of the Martyrs: A Reporter's Journey into Occupied Iraq
—Nir Rosen

Through Our Enemies' Eyes:
Osama bin Laden, Radical Islam, and the Future of America, rev. ed.
—Michael Scheuer

THE
BANALITY
OF
SUICIDE
TERRORISM

The Naked Truth About the Psychology of Islamic Suicide Bombing

NANCY HARTEVELT KOBRIN

FOREWORD BY PHYLLIS CHESLER

Potomac Books, Inc.
Washington, D.C.

Library of Congress Cataloging-in-Publication Data
Kobrin, Nancy.
  The banality of suicide terrorism : the naked truth about the psychology of Islamic suicide bombing / Nancy Hartevelt Kobrin ; foreword by Phyllis Chesler.— 1st ed.
    p. cm.
  Includes bibliographical references and index.
  ISBN 978-1-59797-504-9 (alk. paper)
  1. Suicide bombings—Psychological aspects. 2. Suicide bombers—Psychology. 3. Terrorism—Psychological aspects. 4. Terrorism—Religious aspects—Islam. I. Title.
  HV6431.K625 2010
  363.325—dc22

                                                                    2009039250

Printed in the United States of America on acid-free paper that meets the American National Standards Institute Z39-48 Standard.

Potomac Books, Inc.
22841 Quicksilver Drive
Dulles, Virginia 20166

First Edition

10 9 8 7 6 5 4 3 2 1

In Memory of
Shiri Negari z"l

And all other victims of terrorism, including
Rayhana bint Zayd z"l
Safiya bint Huyay z"l
Maryam Qibtiya
Zainab bint Al-Harith z"l

––––––––––

For my children and grandson, the best teachers I could have

CONTENTS

FOREWORD

The Psychoanalytic Roots of Islamic Suicide Terrorism

If you cherish freedom and the rule of law and if you love both America and Israel, the book you now hold in your hands has the power to potentially save our lives as modern and civilized people. If you work in law enforcement or in the military, Dr. Nancy Kobrin's analysis of Islamic terrorism is an essential and unique weapon. It must be handled with care because many of the psychoanalytic interpretations that she renders will make you feel vulnerable and fearful, both consciously and unconsciously. You may therefore be inclined to resist this information. Please don't. Her work explains the psychology of Al-Qaeda's political serial killer masterminds and their willing recruits.

Dr. Kobrin renames reality for us so that we may better understand it. An Islamic suicide bomber engages in "suicide homicide"; an Islamic kamikaze action is a "cold-blooded, premeditated, group-assisted suicide and homicide." She tells us that a "terrorist" is "terrified"; therefore, he or she "must terrify everyone else."

Dr. Kobrin dares to write about how barbarism is normalized within the Arab and Muslim family. She bravely speaks about "unspeakable" daily realities that are inflicted on children and women but are both hidden and hotly denied. Such childhood and family dynamics lead to a culture in which death is more valued than life. In addition to all the political, military, and economic factors, according to Dr. Kobrin, Islamic suicide terrorism may also be psychologically understood as "displaced rage against (one's) childhood mother," a woman who, after all, has been routinely devalued and battered.

The overall status of women, as well as specific practices such as veiling, sequestration, arranged child marriages, female genital mutilation, polygamy, female illiteracy, stonings, and Arab honor killings, all shape Arab and Muslim psychology and national character. It is important that we pay attention to such Arab and Muslim cultural values in order to understand how they have affected someone like Osama bin Laden for there are more like him where he came from.

Dr. Kobrin draws upon a wealth of knowledge in terms of Arab and Muslim mythology, theology, history, and biography and upon Western psychoanalytic sources. For example, she cites the work of Arno Schmitt and Jehoeda Sofer who published one of the first books in English about the prevalence of male homosexuality in Muslim culture. In Schmitt's preface to the anthology *Sexuality and Eroticism among Males in Moslem Societies*, he suggests that a Muslim boy's "often abrupt rupture" with the female domestic sphere, coupled with his need to both "stand his ground (but at the same time to bow in front of his father and other men in positions of power and respect)," leads to a "precarious male identity."[1]

Based on my own experience in Afghanistan (a non-Arab Muslim culture), as the wife of an Afghan Muslim man, I was an eyewitness to how a polygamous, patriarchal culture also leads to an infernal, fraternal competition for paternal favor and inheritance. It is brother against brother, full brothers against half-brothers, full and half-brothers against first cousins. Thus, entire families and clans can remain locked in revenge-fueled mortal combat for generations.

In this book, Dr. Kobrin bravely tells us that both Arab and Muslim boys and girls are often orally and anally raped by older male relatives, boys between the ages of seven and twelve are publicly and traumatically circumcised, some girls are clitoridectomized, and women are seen as the source of all dishonor and treated accordingly—very, very badly.

Homosexuality, including homosexual pederasty, is apparently as widely prevalent in Islamic societies as it was in ancient Greece. What is taboo, is admitting it. Moreover, the Western concept of being homosexual or gay with all its stigmatized and political-liberatory implications does not exist among Muslims. Muslim society, instead, practices gender apartheid. Thus, in many ways, it is similar to a prison society in which women are kept apart and forbidden and men socialize mainly with each other. Thus, many married fathers have sex with boys and with other men. They do not think of themselves, however, as homosexuals. Homosexuality, especially the act of being penetrated, is forbidden and scorned in Muslim society. As Schmitt puts it:

> A man should not allow others to bugger him. Otherwise, he loses his name, his honor . . . his decisive line is not between the act kept secret and the act known by many, but only talking behind one's back and saying it in your presence, between rumours and public knowledge. . . . As long as nobody draws public attention to something everybody knows, one ignores what might disrupt important social relations.[2]

According to a Human Rights Watch report on Afghanistan, which is cited in Amnesty International's report on Afghanistan, warlords have been known to "routinely sexually molest young boys and to film the orgies."[3]

Carmen Bin Laden revealed, "Homosexuality is forbidden in Saudi Arabia—punished by public flogging. But many men have homosexual relationships, especially when they're young, before they're married. If two men hold hands on the street, as they often do, it's not seen as sexual. . . . The habit of teenage homosexuality doesn't always go away as men age."[4]

The popular novel *The Kite Runner* by Khaled Hosseini depicts Afghan Muslim boys raping another young boy. Hosseini also depicts Taliban-era commanders sexually enslaving young male orphans for orgies and sex murder. But these men, as I noted before, as well as the men whom I saw holding hands and gazing into each other's eyes in Kabul so long ago, were not considered homosexuals.

Throughout the Arab and Muslim world, the male sexual abuse of female children also exists. Indeed, it is one of the main means of traumatizing and shaming girls into obedience and rendering them less capable of resistance or rebellion when they are grown.

Secular, democratic life is foreign to the Arab and Muslim world. Muslims are used to obeying one brutal leader, be it a state tyrant, a clan leader, a particular religious leader, the men of one's own family, and particularly one's father and husband. He often lives more comfortably and has more freedom than his wives and children do; indeed, this distance is a measure of his honor and power. He is nevertheless feared, hated, obeyed, and abjectly adored by his sons, daughters, and wives. This kind of family life may be the psychological template for the relationship between many Muslim people and their political rulers.

In my 1978 book, *About Men*, I posited that the paternal abandonment of and cruelty toward sons may be a crucial component in the mother- and woman-hating culture where women are scapegoated for the crimes of men. Dr. Kobrin also correctly proposes that the absolute degradation of Arab and Muslim women by a shame and honor society means that sons must perpetually rid themselves of the "contamination" that contact with women represents and that sons must also psychologically abandon their mothers. Many sons are trained to mistrust, police, batter, and sometimes murder their female kin—daughters, sisters, cousins, mothers, wives, and so on. Dr. Kobrin believes that such psychological dynamics may play a crucial role in the genesis of Islamic terrorism. According to her, these terrorists harbor a profound fear of being abandoned, which is so great that they must commit in one instant both suicide and mass murder in order to fend off the fear of dependency and abandonment. They literally regress in fantasy and action to the period of early childhood when they were held in the arms of their mothers.

While I agree with Dr. Kobrin, I also want to point out that the exceedingly wealthy male masterminds of suicide terrorism usually neither undertake such missions themselves nor send their biological sons into suicide-homicide martyrdom. They appeal to young men who are not necessarily impoverished or uneducated but who may be starved for a protective alliance with a benevolent father figure—precisely because one does not exist in reality.

Dr. Kobrin uses her considerable skills as a psychoanalyst and as an Arabist to help profile suicide-homicide bombers and their handlers. To the best of my knowledge, she is the first to do this work so comprehensively. For example, together, we worked on "deconstructing" a tape that Osama bin Laden released just before the 2004 U.S. presidential election. In it bin Laden taunts President George W. Bush and tries to shame him in a typical Islamic-Arab technique of punishment, manipulation, and control. Bin Laden declares:

> We never thought the high commander of the U.S. would leave 50,000 of his citizens in both towers to face the horrors by themselves when they most needed him because he thought listening to a child read [this was poorly translated from the Arabic as it had specified a female child] and discussing her goat and its ramming was more important than paying attention to planes and their ramming of the skyscrapers which gave us three times the time to execute the operation, thanks be to God.

He is not telling the truth. Nothing could have stopped the planes.

Osama bin Laden taunted President Bush and America with this tape in the same way that serial killers taunt the police with notes, calls, and the tableaux of the dead that they so carefully stage. But bin Laden's rage is not only tactical, it is also motivated by his early childhood and family dynamics.

Arab and Muslim boys may be traumatized, both sexually and psychologically, but their pride has also been grossly wounded by close ties with a low-status mother and by rivalry with an all-powerful, often sadistic father. First-born sons rarely leave home. They usually remain at home or live nearby and grow old together with everyone they have ever known, including their childhood abusers. Perpetual blood revenge and even human sacrifice—which is what honor murders and clan feuding are really about—help to contain such a non-resolvable set of cultural irritations and hatreds.

Finally, Dr. Kobrin astounded me when she connected the following dots: bin Laden is still psychologically at war with his father, Mohammed, a builder who renovated the famous mosques in Mecca, Medina, and Jerusalem. While Muslims have destroyed and torched mosques, bin Laden has not directly done so. He has, however, destroyed buildings that dared to "tower" over mosques for no infidel, or *dhimmi*, building can be constructed so that it is higher than a Muslim building. What proof do we have for this interesting but arguably dramatic statement? Osama bin Laden's code name for his terrorist attacks are as follows: the attack on Kenya was known as the Holy Ka'aba (which is in Mecca), and the attack on Tanzania was known as the Al-Aqsa (which is in Jerusalem).

Dr. Kobrin and I have worked on a series of articles together. I have learned from her tremendously. We have been told that our work—which is largely based on her research and understanding of terrorism—has already helped save lives in the line of fire. It has been my privilege to serve with her in this capacity.

Phyllis Chesler, PhD
New York City, 2009

PREFACE

Why is this book needed now? Islamic suicide terrorism is on the rise. More and more innocent civilians—men, women, and children—are being murdered every day in cold blood by Islamic terrorist groups that deploy suicide bombers.

As I was beginning to write this book, many events informed my thinking about suicide terrorism and political domestic violence pertaining to Islam. First, the Dutch Islamic terrorist Muhammad Bouyeri brutally murdered Theo van Gogh in November 2004 on an Amsterdam street. It was reported that Bouyeri had become a born-again Muslim fanatic after his mother's death. Obviously he had problems concerning his mother that preceded his brutal butchering of Theo Van Gogh. Bouyeri felt bitter and abandoned by her when she died. He acted out his murderous rage for her on van Gogh. Bouyeri also hated van Gogh for making a scathing movie entitled *Submission*, which was critical of Islam's treatment of women and unconsciously reminded Bouyeri of his own pathological dependency on his *ummi* (mommy).

Working with a Syrian terrorist group, Bouyeri meant to terrorize Dutch officials and the entire European community along with the viewers of the global media. The Dutch Somali and ex-Muslim member of parliament Ayaan Hirsi Ali had written the movie's script, which was based on her life story. It included fleeing an arranged marriage with a cousin, domestic violence, and female circumcision at age five. The confluence of Muslim domestic violence and political domestic violence of Islamic suicide terrorism occurred under the guise of van Gogh's political assassination. Hirsi Ali was then forced into hiding and then exile.

Within the same month Margaret Hassan, the director of the international humanitarian organization Cooperative for Assistance and Relief Everywhere, Inc. (CARE), was assassinated as well in Iraq. The cold-blooded murder is transparent. The Islamic terrorists murdered her precisely because she cared. The international media ran pictures of her with an infant in her arms à la the maternal cameo. Hassan was the embodiment of maternal nurturing and solicitude, something the terrorists do not understand. Feeling depleted and envious, they murdered this innocent woman.

Then came Abu Musab al-Zarqawi and his cruel beheadings. I have heard no one else linking these murders to Zarqawi's becoming unglued by the death of his mother, Dallah Ibrahim Mohammed al-Khalayleh, known by her *kunya* (first-born son) as Um Sayel. After a long illness, she died on February 29, 2004, from leukemia. Almost to the fortieth day of Muslim mourning known as *arbeen*, her son, whom I will call the Sheikh of Killers, abducted Nicholas Berg on April 9 and beheaded him on May 11. Berg's was the first of a long series of hostages' executions. Ironically, it was as if Zarqawi—who hated the Shi'a—was engaged in the Shiite religious holiday called Arbeen, which occurs forty days after Ashura, or the commemoration of the martyrdom by beheading of Husayn bin Ali, the Prophet Muhammad's grandson, on the plains of Karbala in A.D. 680. Ayatollah Ruhollah Khomeini, adopting a leading ideologue's slogan for the Iranian Revolution, once said: "Every place should be turned into Karbala, every month into Moharram and every day into Ashura."[1] Surely every beheading, most especially the almost certain decapitation of the walking suicide bomber, recapitulates this slogan. Under normal circumstances in Islam, the period of forty days—also called literally by the Arabic word for forty, *arbeen*—is the traditional time of mourning. During this sacred time, Muslims are not supposed to engage in crime, especially murder, and it is as if Zarqawi contained his rage while he mourned his mother. Then he lost it and went on his rampage.

There is a profound lack of understanding of the psychodynamics of this particular kind of political violence. This book attempts to explain these terrorists' core terrors—specifically, they are terrified to separate from their mothers psychologically and remain fused with them, which binds and blinds them. This book is not meant to blame the mothers; rather, it attempts to explain this unique mother-child relationship. The Arab Muslim culture in which they live has not permitted their children to grow up into confident and competent adults. Not being allowed to separate psychologically leaves their children feeling distrustful and terrified of the outside world and induces an inordinate amount of persecutory anxieties.

The complex behavior of suicide terrorism is in the initial stage of being understood; its surface has only been scratched. Terrorist behavior is primarily predatory; therefore, the "animal" in the human needs to be examined as well along with its nonverbal communication. To quote Tom Hunt: "We are the only animals that can hate, blame, and shame ourselves, envision a bleak future, question the meaning of life, and imagine our own death."[2] Science tells us that "the social environment in which the pregnant mother is located" is vital to the baby's development and most especially to that of the baby's mind.[3]

It is vitally important to understand Arab Muslim culture in all its diversity as it is the baby's social environment. We are only at the very beginning of this project. A small portion is the development of a theory about the murderous rage that the terrorists harbor against the prenatal mother. They are clueless as to what they tell us about themselves through their nonverbal behaviors. They do not recognize that all behavior is potentially meaningful.

To the best of my knowledge, my "Early Mother" theory, which is related to British Object Relations theory, is the first to date that seeks to explain the meaning of the brutal imagery of the Islamic suicide attack scene as a crime scene by focusing on the death fusion of the suicide bomber and his or her victims. This theory is not meant to serve as a predictor for who will become a suicide bomber and who will choose not to do so. Rather, it is intended to provide a deeper understanding behind the roots of terrorism by focusing on its participants' behavior. Again, all behavior is potentially meaningful.

In this book I am describing terrorism and suicide bombing from a linguistic psychosocial and psychohistorical perspective as a psychoanalyst whose clinical expertise is in posttraumatic stress disorders and whose life experience has been formed by studying many languages and cultures, including Arabic and Aljamía (Old Spanish in Arabic), for my doctorate. This book might conceivably shed some light on a frequently asked question: why does someone become a suicide bomber? Once again, though, it is not the book's main intent or focus.

Since this work is new and innovative, in reviewing the literature I have not found much material relating to the subject of imagery and terrorism. Like a computer sleuth, I have had to "hack the system" of a vast body of literature in order to piece together a theory, and I have referred to numerous authors, both psychoanalytically oriented and not, throughout the book.

Hopefully these chapters provide a story line that is internally consistent with the terrorists' mind-set and, hence, helps to explain the external event of the suicide attack's crime scene rather than obscure it. Here, it is determined the terrorists have impaired thinking because they lack a maturity stemming from independence. Until now, moreover, no theoretical link has been made between the violence they have learned in the home and the imagery of the political violence of their suicide terrorism as it relates to the question of women in general and the "Early Mother" in particular.

Finally, a word on spelling: I have not attempted a scientific transcription for Arabic words. I follow my own preference for transcription for non-English words. There is no standard method for Arabic. With regard to proper names, I have chosen the common spellings in English translation, as in the case of the name of the Prophet Muhammad and the organization of Al-Qaeda.

ACKNOWLEDGMENTS

For a long time I have been thinking about the subject of terrorism, but I didn't have the network of support to tackle such a complex and intricate area. Therefore, I have many people to thank, for each one played a specific role to this contribution to the literature. First and foremost, I must express my gratitude to my colleague Yoram Schweitzer (www.labat.co.il), who is Israel's leading counterterrorism expert on Al-Qaeda. He was the first to identify Osama bin Laden as a threat to the West.

Through his seminar on suicide terrorism given by the Jaffee Center for Strategic Studies at Tel Aviv University I met Reuven Paz, PhD, the director of the Project on Radical Islamist Movements (PRISM, at www.eprism.org.il) and the former director of research for the Shin Bet, Israel, for fifteen years. Reuven was the first scholar fluent in both spoken and written Arabic (the latter being virtually unheard of for a non-Arab speaker). Without hesitation he read this book manuscript and offered his encouragement to go forward and get it published. In addition, he invited me to present my work at the Interdisciplinary Center for Counter-Terrorism in Herzliya, Israel, in September 2005, where I provided an overview of a new and original theory of "imagery" to explain the Islamic suicide attack as a hybrid of a crime scene related to serial killing by proxy, domestic violence's murder-suicide, and honor killing. Subsequently, I have revised it for this book as well as for a North Atlantic

Treaty Organization (NATO) Advanced Research Workshop in December 2006.

Special thanks go to Professor Yitzhak Reiter who generously took his time out of a busy schedule to critique the text. As a scholar of Islam and of Arab culture, his insights and comments have been invaluable.

The war on terrorism is not only a war of words (for which it has been said that "when it comes to the battle of ideas, the U.S. has no general").[1] More important, it is a war of imagery, according to a research team from Radio Free Europe/Radio Liberty's study "Iraqi Insurgent Media: The War of Images and Ideas" by Daniel Kimmage and Kathleen Ridolfo and cited in the *Wall Street Journal*.[2] This concept is a new and imaginative way to view and explain the meaning of the imagery found at the site of the suicide attack. Yet to date, there has been no theory of imagery to explain the suicide attack site and its psychological "site."

A very special thanks is in order to Joan Lachkar, PhD (www.joanlach-karphd.com), for her invaluable insights concerning psychoanalysis and psychohistory. She has been instrumental in helping me conceptualize many of the unanswered questions that need to be raised and posed. I also wish to thank Avner Falk, PhD, for his expertise concerning psychohistory and psychobiography, particularly with regard to the Arab-Israeli conflict.

A special tribute goes to Dr. Phyllis Chesler who was instrumental in making this book a reality. Oddly, we had our initial meeting through the Internet. This eminent matriarch of the second wave of feminism is the renowned author of more than thirteen books (www.phyllis-chesler.com), including *Women and Madness, Revised* (Palgrave Macmillan, 2005); *The New Anti-Semitism: The Current Crisis and What We Must Do about It* (Jossey-Bass, 2003); *The Death of Feminism: What's Next in the Struggle for Women's Freedom* (Palgrave Macmillan, 2006); and her most recent book, *Woman's Inhumanity to Woman, Revised* (Lawrence Hill Books, 2009). Phyllis took great interest in my manuscript without even having met me and thereby gave credence to the material presented herein. She has spent tireless hours helping me get this manuscript to a publishing house. I am honored that she introduces the book.

At the same time, Sander Breiner, MD—a psychoanalyst in Michigan, an expert on child sacrifice, and the author of *Slaughter of the Innocents: Child Abuse through the Ages and Today* (Plenum Press, 1990)—also read the manuscript and encouraged me to pursue publication.

At this point, Phyllis then decided to write about the book's manuscript at *FrontPageMag.com*. Because of her article, the U.S. Army requested to read the manuscript, and I gave permission to the army to use it as the army saw fit in the war on terrorism. Phyllis Chesler and I were told that it was being used in psyops, which is a special field of psychological warfare. To paraphrase Sun Tzu, the ancient philosopher of war, we must know our enemy, which means that we must know their core terrors as well. This book represents this special, seldom explored terrain of terrorism.

It was heartwarming to know both that my book manuscript has been put to use by the military and that by making the conflict more understandable and thus leading to less use of deadly force, it has saved lives—odd as that may seem—in what has been, and continues to be, a protracted conflict. A U.S. Army contact (who cannot be mentioned by name) related to me something very important about my theory. In the early 1990s, he served with a British Special Forces commander who taught military analysts and conducted special operations. The commander emphasized that Islamic suicide terrorism was just like domestic violence: terrorists are "seeking the dehumanization and depersonalization of the enemy." Indeed, his words were prophetic as suicide attacks have since become as commonplace and routine as are the murder-suicides of domestic violence. In mid-2007, Benazir Bhutto wrote, "For the first time in Pakistan's history, the number of religious-based parties is rising, and suicide bombings are becoming a common occurrence of daily life."[3] She herself was assassinated in a suicide bombing on December 27, 2007.

I offered to give a seminar to graduating military intelligence officers of the U.S. Army. I went on my own dime and arrived at 1:30 a.m. in the sleepy town of St. Robert near Fort Leonard Wood, Missouri. I received no honorarium for this lecture yet I felt honored. I wanted to meet in person those who were using my work. I had the privilege of giving the last seminar of a two-week intensive course concerning military intelligence to first-level army officers. It was nothing short of an amazing experience. I met the other instructors and continue to be in contact with them. They have provided excellent support, including having the faith that this book would see the light of day.

In addition to the U.S. Army, I also wish to thank Maj. Donald Palmer, USAF, the director of the Middle East Orientation Course for Special Operations, in Hurlburt Field, Florida, for the opportunity to present a seminar on the psychology of extremism—specifically, of the suicide bombers and their gender issues. Shortly thereafter I met Lt. Col. Guermantes Lailari, USAF, a gifted linguist and cryptologist with expertise concerning suicide terrorism who has also been immensely helpful. I also wish to thank Gen. Montgomery Meigs, USA, who took my request—to go down range and experience the battlefield firsthand in order to understand the use of the improvised explosive devices (IEDs)—and my work seriously.

This book would not have seen the light of day if it hadn't been for Dr. Anat Berko, who put me in touch with Potomac Books, Inc. Furthermore, it was Dr. Berko who urged me to incorporate the word "proxy" for suicide bombings as serial killings by proxy. A mutual colleague, Abe Wagner, also invited me to present at Rand in May 2008. I remain profoundly indebted to Dr. Berko.

There are a series of people to be thanked whose help allowed me to refine my theory. Special thanks go to Jamie Glazov at FrontPageMag.com, where I have had the opportunity to publish my thoughts and engage in challenging symposia concerning terrorism.

Others who offered expertise and help are Norman Simms, PhD; Daphna Blacksea; Doris Brothers, PhD; Niki Anderson; Marilyn Stern; Robbie Friedmann, PhD; Rex Hudson, PhD; Boaz Ganor, PhD; Gloria Burgess Levine, PhD; Margaret Fulton, PhD; Marv Logel, PhD; Dayna Anderson, MA; Ellen Luepker, MSW; Head Librarian Mary Wittenberg and Associate Librarian Jennifer Feeken at Regions Hospital Medical Library; and Sheriff Patrick D. McGowen and his staff, including Helen Klun, Sgt. Lynn Miller, Lt. Jeff

Schlumpberger, Lieutenant Peterson, Lt. Connie Meyer, and Deputies Tim McGough, David L. Schultz, and Jeanine Brudenell.

Farther afield were many other scholars who helped along the way. The manuscript was originally six hundred pages in length, and many helpful comments did not make it into the final version. Nonetheless, they helped: Martin Strohmeier, PhD; Angela Zerbe and Laila Yalcin-Hekmann, PhD; Bill Fierman, PhD; Zev Alexander, MD; Moshe Gammer, PhD; Alex Bialsky; David Meir-Lev; Robert Spencer of Jihad Watch; Yaniv Ofek; Professor Mordechai Kedar; Jason Post; Andrew Bostom, MD; Daphne Burdman, MD; Professor Nick Spadaccini and Professor Joseba Zulaika; Xabier Unanume; Professor Florentino Portero; Dr. Juan Aviles; Dr. Luisa Baron Hernández; and most especially Isaac Martín-Barbero, who wrote an excellent editorial on my behalf when another publisher abruptly dropped my book from publication. Jeff Denning deserves special thanks for all of his ongoing support, having written about the book at *FrontPageMag.com* at a critical time. May Samra, editor of *Magen David Magazine* of Mexico, interviewed me about my work early on, and I wish to thank her for her support. While I do not personally know Amir Taheri, he too was kind enough to cite the book fiasco in an editorial piece as well. I am especially indebted to Arjuna Gunawardena who gave me a crash course on the Liberation Tigers of Tamil Eelam (LTTE) terrorism while in Sri Lanka.

Thanks also go to my editor, Deana Deck, and to my bibliographer who wished to remain anonymous. Both of them were gems to work with. I am profoundly grateful to the editorial staff at Potomac Books, Inc., who made invaluable enhancements to my book, especially Hilary Claggett.

Special thanks are warranted and extended to Gail and Irv Handelman; Ina Leiserson; Meira and Dani Idan; Nancy and Jerry Rauch; Liz and Marty Swaden; Judith and Jerome Ingber; Carlos Schenck, MD, and Andrea Murphy Schenck; Sandi and David Lior, MD; Sofia and Alex Pisarenko; Susan and Harold Kudler, MD; and Paul Wagner.

I am indebted to my former husband's Israeli family and especially to cousin Orit Kishon for all their support. Others who provided support and might not have been aware include Shira Ozeri (hayahalom b'keter shel ha-sokhnut); Barbara Hyer, MD; Dianne Hanson; Deborah Shatin; Jill Kaskinen; Professor David Bunis; Gary and Nina Wexler; Vivian Fink, MD; and Rabbi Alan Shavit-Lonstein. I think of and wish to thank my most formative teachers: Professor Antônio Andrade, Rabbi Professor Byron Sherwin, Professor Tzioni Zevit, Professor Mayer Gruber, the late Professor Anwar Chejne, Professor Yonatan Paradise, and Professor Wladyslaw Godzich. There were others whose memory kept me going: Lindy Goldstone z"l; Nat London, MD, z"l; and Aunt Florence Cohen z"l.

Finally, I wish to inscribe my very special thanks and my profound love and gratitude to my children and my grandson. I am so very fortunate to have had their love and support during the writing of this book. Nonetheless, I assume full responsibility for its contents, and any errors that may occur are solely mine.

ACKNOWLEDGMENTS FOR ESSAYS

I wish to acknowledge and thank the following editors and journals in which some of these chapters first appeared. All of these book chapters have been rewritten. Chapter 2 was previously published as an article, "Imitation of Judaism," in *Clio's Psyche* (September 2002).

An earlier version of chapter 3 first appeared as "The Death Pilots of September 11th, 2001: The Ultimate Schizoid Dilemma" in *Jihad and Sacred Vengeance*, volume 3 of *Psychological Undercurrents of History Volume* (Writers Club Press, 2002). This chapter received the International Society for Psychohistory award for innovative thinking. I am indebted to the book's editors: Drs. Jerry Piven, Christopher Boyd, and Henry Lawton.

Chapter 4 first appeared in "A Psychoanalytic Approach to bin Laden, Political Violence, and Islamic Suicidal Terrorism," *Clio's Psyche* (2002). I wish to thank the editors—Professor Paul Elovitz and Professor Bob Lentz. This chapter won the Minnesota Association for Marriage and Family Therapy (MAMFT) Editor's Award upon its publication. It appeared in a reprinted, abridged version in *MAMFT News: The Newsletter of the Minnesota Associa-*

tion for Marriage and Family Therapy (September 2002). I wish to thank Dr. Ken Stewart for his support.

Chapter 5 appeared in 2002 as "Psychoanalytic Notes on Osama bin Laden and His Jihad against the Jews and the Crusaders," *The Annual of Psychoanalysis* (2002). I wish to thank Dr. James Anderson and Dr. Jerome Winer.

Chapter 7 was first published online as "Political Serial Killing by Proxy: Christian Ganczarski the Chief Perpetrator, Nizar Nawar His Proxy, and the Djerba Synogogue Bombing," in *Anil Aggrawal's Internet Journal of Forensics and Toxicology* (December 2007). I am greatly indebted to Dr. Anil Aggrawal and his ongoing support. I wish to thank Ian Johnson, former Berlin bureau chief of the *Wall Street Journal,* for having kindly provided me with a portion of the German police deposition of Christian Ganczarski that deals with his early childhood. I wish to also thank my former doctoral student, Dr. David Van Dyke, for his excellent translation of this document and other insightful comments. For the original, please consult the online version, which quotes portions of the German deposition in translation at www.geradts.com/anil/ij/vol_008_no_002/papers/paper001.html. On account of this essay and the use of the German police deposition, I was contacted by France's leading counterterrorism expert, Jean-Charles Brisard, who at the time I was writing this book was preparing the legal team to prosecute Christian Ganczarski and his Al-Qaeda cohorts. I was honored to learn that this essay might be helpful in the legal arena as only the law's analysis and interpretation of a question are binding on a community.

1

THE MOTHER'S SHAME AND THE TERRORIST'S BLAME

It is better to die with honor than live with humiliation.
—Arabic saying

Islamic suicide terrorism can be understood as a new variant of an old problem—domestic violence—that has existed since time immemorial across many cultures. Islamic suicide terrorism gives a new, complicated twist to domestic violence because that is where conjoint murder and suicide routinely occur. Islamic suicide terrorism merits the name of political domestic violence because it is a military political tool used by radical political Islam as well as by secular Muslim terrorist organizations. Each suicide bombing attack thus constitutes a crime scene.

This exploration of Islamic terrorism is focused specifically on the cultural influences that motivate the terrorist. Millions of Muslims lead peaceful lives, so what happens that influences those few who elect to become suicide bombers? We still do not know precisely who will become a terrorist and why, but we can work backward from the crime scene and surmise its psychodynamics through what it communicates. Where you have a devalued woman and an overidealized mother, as you do in Arab and Muslim cultures, and where there is a prohibition to separate from the mother, such violent problems as murder-suicide may ensue.

The status of the woman in these cultures is complex. To quote Laurie Brand, and to apply her observation from the Jordanian context to the broader Arab and Muslim world, is relevant:

> Given that women's status in the Arab world is generally attributed to Islam, how should one then interpret the present status of women in Jordan? The discussion here does not deny the importance of Islam to legislation and to more general societal mores in the kingdom which affect women and their status. Nevertheless, understanding the place of women in any Islamic society requires an examination of the interaction of a complex set of factors, of which Islam is only one. Over time, any religion is interwoven with or conditioned by the structures and traditions of the society into which it is introduced . . . in the discussion of law, not just sharia, but also 'urf (traditional tribal or village law) plays a key role in Jordan. The state's reliance on the tribes, and its cultivation of them through the provision of various forms of patronage, has strongly reinforced the importance of tribal values and norms in Jordanian society, whether they are actually codified in law or not. Neither the state nor the Islamists have sought to exorcise the impact of 'urf from Jordanian law. Indeed many average Jordanians do not distinguish between sharia and 'urf, instead believing that all current practice is demanded by Islam.[1]

From a psychoanalytic perspective, teasing out the different cognitive, artificially constructed linguistic categories such as sharia and 'urf becomes less problematic because the focus on the engine driving the violence does not care about such categories. They are emotionally lived beliefs. Indeed, it is a good philosophical, defensive, rationalized fantasy that one can compartmentalize the ideologies separately from the lethal behaviors.

This point is relevant because Al-Qaeda emphasizes Islam. Al-Qaeda members, however, have not hesitated to kill and murder their fellow Muslims even during the month of Ramadan. Why should this fact be surprising? In domestic violence, killing one's own family members is a common occurrence. Sectarian suicide terrorism is no different as it is a form of murder within one's "extended" family, namely, the nation-state.

Ironically, all the Islamic terrorist groups that have deployed suicide bombers—even those using female bombers—are male dominated. The title of a recent film concerning two Pakistani Muslims who become radical Islamists and then choose to carry out suicide bombings in New York captures their internal psychosexual conflict. Externalized, projected outward, and ultimately in one instance enacted as a suicide bombing, their inner struggles are represented in *The War Within*.[2] The title precisely reflects the men's case, as the war is within the self; but the suicide bombers and their terrorist organizations are also embattled with the world. To counter Islamic suicide terrorism, then, one must recognize the core terrors of the terrorists as well as our own terrors: the terrors are about the mother. Since everyone has a mother, terrorism taps into the oldest, most archaic terrors that everyone relates to consciously or unconsciously. The suicide bombing attack accesses this immediate, nonverbal, and visceral communicative circuit that connects humanity.

This book explains Islamic suicide terrorism as displaced rage against the "Early Mother" of childhood because the young mother in these cultures has been so utterly devalued, abused, and traumatized as a child that when she becomes a mother, often at a young age, she is compromised. She struggles in her capacity to mother in a completely unsupported environment in which she is further abused.

Anwar Hekmat, an expert on the Quran and its treatment of women, shows that wife beating is justified in the Muslim family because it is stated explicitly in the Quran. Children who witness their mother being beaten experience it as a direct attack on themselves because they are psychologically dependent on their mother and feel that a part of themselves resides in her. Beating the mother is a tactic in the psychological warfare of the home to get the child to submit to the father's will. It therefore constitutes child abuse. Tawfik Hamid stresses that, according to the Hadith, the Prophet Muhammad instructed children to be beaten into praying at the age of ten.[3] It is an attempt on the part of the father, who has been absent until that time, to gain power and control. Not all children who are beaten, however, grow up to be serial killers or serial killers by proxy, that is, sent by terrorist organizations to act as suicide bombers.

Islamic suicide terrorism is informed by the child's experience that violence and force are to be used as a means to control others. It is learned behavior, which is ingrained early in life.

One writer reports that the Islamic terrorist operative is routinely described as "an upstanding citizen," a "loving husband," and even a "gentle father."[4] But relatively few outside of the Arab Muslim world know what really takes place behind closed doors at home. Many examples of abusive family life are found in current literature. As mentioned above, wife beating is mandated in the Quran. In her book *The Trouble with Islam: A Muslim's Call for Reform in Her Faith*, Irshad Manji relates witnessing her father routinely beating her mother. In another work, Phyllis Chesler recounts how a former Palestine Liberation Organization (PLO) terrorist who left Islam spoke of his father's brutal treatment of his mother and his battering of her.[5] In 2004 Rania al-Baz, the prominent Saudi television talk show hostess, went public with her husband's brutal beating that left her with thirteen facial fractures. She was instantly fired from her job.

In Arab Muslim culture, the mother plays the central role in child rearing during the earliest years, but she should not be blamed for creating terrorists and suicide bombers. She herself is a victim. It will be shown that the terrorists are the result of the regrettable abuse and devaluation of women and girls in Arab Muslim culture. This treatment leaves the mother with little freedom. She only experiences her omnipotent self as the powerful center of her baby's universe. The mother's feeling of empowerment recycles the abuse and shaming techniques that she herself experienced as a devalued girl child. She thereby communicates a sense of worthlessness even to her baby son, who is still overly prized and valued. He also is raised having more prerogatives than a little girl will ever have.

Moreover, the male child is abruptly taken from the world of his mother at the age of seven by his father and joins the society of men. The gradual separation of the child from his mother, which usually begins to occur in puberty, never takes place. His realization of himself as an individual, his sense of emotional independence that such individuation provides, and his formation of a mature intelligence are thus all stunted.

This psychological loss is significant and frightening. It too relies upon shaming techniques stemming from the father's authority, which is based on terror. There is also intense sibling rivalry among males in some Muslim families that is coupled with the strategy of humiliating the sons, which a father does in order to defend as well as further define his own patriarchal position and sense of masculinity within the family. He pits the sons against each other, leaving them subordinated and shamed. It is the same pattern and dynamic encountered with the father's wives, who must vie to see who will be his "chosen" one.

In a family where the mother is routinely abused and dominated, there is little for a child to respect. In Arab Muslim families, children are not considered as individual personalities, and their unquestioning obedience to their father is demanded. They can expect severe punishment for any act of disobedience. Because of the father's unapproachable authority, the children grow up clinging to and dependent on their insignificant mother, factors that can lead to the formation of a constricted self. As noted, young boys are removed from their mother's sphere of influence at an early age. They then join the company of men or, more likely, that of their older siblings, cousins, half brothers, and even uncles young enough to be their brothers. Older brothers wield power within the household second only to that of the patriarch. As in all families, there is a good deal of abusive behavior toward younger siblings, a wolf pack mentality as it were, as the boys sort out who is "king of the hill" or the alpha male. For boys brought up in homes where physical and sexual abuse are the norm, it follows that they copy the behavior of their fathers and older male relatives, passing the abusive treatment along to the younger, most vulnerable children.

With no mother capable of protecting them and an overbearing, brutal father blind to their needs, such children may grow up feeling helpless and enraged. They have no recourse but to fight back. When they mature and fall under the influence of religious zealots and the experienced handlers of Al-Qaeda, they become prime candidates for exploitation.

CHILD-REARING PRACTICES

As reported by the United Nations (UN) Educational, Scientific, and Cultural Organization (UNESCO), internationally recognized experts, many of whom are Muslims, have noted that there are high rates of child sexual abuse in the Arab Muslim world. More than fifty Muslim countries have endorsed this international organization's findings, thereby acknowledging professionally that Arab and Muslim child-rearing practices are not up to acceptable international norms of human behavior.

Arab Muslim culture is not one in which children are loved and hugged appropriately. Important researchers such as Lila Abu-Lughod, Halim Barakat, and Hisham Sharabi have noted the repression of children in a culture in which rage and anger are valued over love and healthy, balanced affection. Howard Bloom calls this critical absence of healthy affection "the importance of hugging." Bloom poses the key observation:

> In much of Arab society, the unmerciful approach of fathers to their children continues, and public warmth between men and women is still considered an evil. Perhaps this is why a disproportionate number of Arab adults, stripped of intimacy and thrust into a life in which vulnerable emotion is a sin, have joined extremist movements dedicated to wreaking havoc on the world.[6]

Arab Muslim culture is a shame-based culture. It is not the first culture to be described as such, however; Japan was cited as a shame-based culture during World War II. A shame-based culture is male dominated and patriarchal, with the shaming dependent upon abusive child-rearing practices. To a child, an abuser is a terrorist. Michael Johnson discovered that there was a higher rate of abuse found in patriarchal homes and even coined the expression "patriarchal terrorism."[7] According to the United Nations Children's Fund (UNICEF), child abuse routinely occurs in the Arab world. Not every person coming from a shame-based culture will become a terrorist, just as not every abused child in America, a permissive culture by contrast, becomes an abuser. Nevertheless, how a child is treated during childhood may determine how he or she chooses to treat others later in life. This observation is conventional wisdom.

The question of what makes a person become a terrorist, and especially a suicide bomber, is complex in many ways. Is it nurture versus nature? Are genes and biochemistry involved, causing one to become so violent? Is it only a matter of child-rearing practices? Most likely it is multifactorial. Admittedly, the question cannot be answered as precisely as we would like at this time. Trying to figure out the motivations of a suicide bomber beyond his or her use as a tactical tool in a terrorist organization's arsenal involves many different strands. Gathering different expert opinions together into an integrated model concerning this phenomenon remains in the early stages, with the study of modern suicide terrorism still in its infancy. If we were to compare the state of current research to a car, the experts are driving a Model T Ford. Nevertheless, in *Ghosts from the Nursery: Tracing the Roots of Violence*, Robin Karr-Morse and Meredith Wiley have shown that the roots of violence are found in early childhood experience for American children. It should be possible to explore early childhood for the Arab Muslim child as well and ponder how that experience might relate to the explosion of Muslim terrorists worldwide.

Some aspects are evident. For example, a child who is loved and well cared for in an appropriate way by his or her mother (and father) does not grow up to be a suicide bomber or an operative in a terrorist organization like Al-Qaeda. A child who is loved, no matter what level of education or economic class, does not murder himself or herself and others. A child who has been abused and manipulated, however, is at risk of committing the mass murder of suicide bombings even though most abused children who become adults choose not to murder. The focus should not be solely placed on the suicide bomber, as it is not the suicide bomber per se who is the exclusive problem. Joan Lachkar, an expert on abuse, stresses that the broader issue for suicide terrorism involves the notions of sacrifice; the attitudes of the self, the other, and the group toward life and death, Eros, honor and shame; and so on. Getting revenge by becoming a suicide bomber and by being an operative who participates in a terrorist organization that produces suicide bombers becomes a more pervasive force than life itself.

The dysfunctional family has not previously been taken into account for the suicide attack. It is not within the scope of this book to explain how suicide terrorism spreads, but suffice it to say that many children grow up in shame or honor cultures where they are not affectionately related to in an appropriate way and share other commonalities with such cultures as the Tamil Tigers and the Japanese kamikazes. It is one factor among a series but an important one. As the suicide attacker's rageful flames of immolation are ignited, they spread across diverse cultures through converts to Islam as well.

There are high rates of female infant mortality in the Arab world, resulting from neglect and maltreatment, with male babies receiving better treatment. International consensus concerning acceptable standards of behavior has facilitated an ongoing inquiry into this most sensitive area. In stark contradiction, the United Nations also recognizes polygamy as a "legitimate form of marriage and allows its employees to divide benefits among more than one wife."[8] In cultures that condone polygamy, husbands have many wives. The practice is known to be a means of pathologically controlling females and constitutes a form of abuse that, instead, should be an indicator of a human rights violation. Moreover, scientific studies conducted in the Arab world—by Arabs—have demonstrated the negative effects of the practice and have concluded that it causes mental illness.[9]

MAGICAL THINKING, BLAMING, AND VERBAL THREATS

S. J. Breiner, who has written extensively about child-rearing practices in the Middle East, stresses the persistence of "magical thinking," which is further associated with a child's feeling of powerlessness. According to Breiner, "Even though there is a sense of fatalism in that everything is Allah's will, there is a lot of wishful thinking and the belief in magic, the evil eye and the powerful Jinn."[10] This superstition of sorts leads one to avoid dealing with reality and aggression. Some Arabists are adamant about maintaining a distinction between Arab culture and Muslim culture to the point that they think of two different, coexisting worlds—the first being the Arab, numbering around 300 million people, and the second being Muslim, which is estimated to number from 1.2 to 1.5 billion people. Despite their differences, together they tend to be referred to as the *umma*, or the Arab Muslim world. Henceforth, I will refer to both of these worlds as the Arab Muslim world. It is too easy, otherwise, to hide behind the linguistic constructs of where either culture begins and ends. They are intricately intertwined, which further complicates the problem. Referring to the cultures as the Arab Muslim world does not allow one to use philosophical arguments that "blame" Arab culture rather than dealing with how the ideologies of Islam fit hand in glove with the normalized bad behavior found in that culture. Furthermore, Arab culture—as found in Saudi Arabia— is *the* venerated culture for the Muslims. In addition, moderate Muslims refuse to take a stance against extreme blood violence. The majority of Muslims allows others to be the carriers of its disavowed rage and to act it out. The Arab Muslim world tends to participate in inciting the political violence by turning a blind eye to it.

Magical thinking makes it difficult, if not impossible, for a group to assume responsibility for its actions. Inaction is denied because the very word— that is, just speaking the word itself—in the Arabic language takes on special meaning and is viewed as an actual deed even if the deed has never happened. Talking, therefore, is synonymous with doing. This idea is the essence of magical thinking.

All Arabs feel themselves to be brothers or as a part of *Dar al Islam* (House or Territories of Islam) versus *Dar al Harb* (House or Territories of War, literally the "sword," or the non-Muslim world that is to be conquered either by the sword or by conversion). Being embattled is a way of life in

Islam. There is always one war or another going on, either in the home or in the greater society. This state is corroborated by the use of physical violence on children. To quote Breiner:

> Generally speaking the Arab world makes more frequent use of harsher forms of corporal punishment with their children than is found in the West. Fathers are seen as severe, stern and frightening to their children. While the children respect their fathers, they fear them and tend to have more affection and attachment to their depreciated mothers. However, the mothers tend to approve of the harsh punishing of their children, particularly the boys, and they think it much more acceptable for the fathers to be severe than to not be severe. Those fathers who are harsh to their children in punishment also tend to be severe and harsh in hitting their wives.[11]

Jihadis, or those who wage holy war, are born into a Muslim family, which is their first experience in a group. Others do convert and become radicalized (see chapter 7), as John Walker Lindh did. Later on, the jihadis' surrogate family is the terrorist organization. The early terrors in life are reexperienced later in the terrorist group, a highly enmeshed and fused entity. Even the loners came from families, and their radicalization precisely tells us that they lacked a sustaining and meaningful connection with their own families. Even though these families may claim to the media that their sons and daughters who became terrorists are really sweet, kind, and normal people, this assertion should be doubted and treated skeptically since their culture of shame has so infused the group's sensitivity to criticism. They must always present a good face to the public because they feel so excruciatingly shamed. Vamik Volkan, the renowned Turkish Cypriot psychoanalyst who is a Muslim, has repeatedly asserted that in Arab Muslim culture, there is a socialized need to hate and have an enemy, and it is learned behavior in the home.[12] This situation is further complicated, Halim Barakat notes, by the fact that in Arab culture the love-hate relationship is predicated on scaring tactics (*at-tarhib*) and enticement (*at-targhib*). These two dynamics, when entwined, add fuel to the fire of sadomasochism that pervades jihadi culture and its violence.[13]

Child-rearing practices that are grounded in abuse complicate the quest for a sustained family connection. Abuse brutalizes the concept of connection and contaminates it. In Western culture, it has been shown that abused children—though not all, of course—tend to abuse pets in childhood and often grow up to be abusive spouses and parents. We should never give up hope, however, that some will come through such a brutalizing experience and seek to behave differently.

I have developed and coined a series of terms in order to describe this disavowed psychological undercurrent and its routes and roots that especially pertain to Islamic suicide terrorism. Three of these concepts are "political, domestic violence's murder-suicide"; the "maternal cameo"; and "political serial killing by proxy." I am indebted to Dr. Anat Berko for encouraging me to adopt the word "proxy" to describe this last phenomenon.

The Islamic suicide attack is a hybrid of domestic violence's murder-suicide, serial killing, and the Arab clan custom of honor killing. That there is no word for honor killing or suicide bombing in Arabic is more than just happenstance. Moreover, Arabic has no word for homosexuality.[14] The Arab Muslims have chosen to deny that honor killing is cold-blooded murder and that suicide bombing is mass slaughter of the innocent.

Honor killing is itself a misnomer since it has nothing to do with honor. It exclusively targets women and girls. My colleague Dr. Chesler rightly refers to it as "honor murder." Unfortunately, some authors fail to name honor killing for what it really is—the slaughter of a female in cold blood:

> Once we realize this fact [that honor killing has to do with only the woman], we discover the misinterpretation of the meaning of honor. The noble values of dignity and seniority are neglected. Instead, the only focus is on the woman's body and her virginity. According to this definition, the woman is an object owned by the man who assumes responsibility for her behavior and her life. The social traditions lead to the

isolation of the woman in her home. She is required to cover her entire body in order to maintain the honor of the man. A decent honorable man has to have a woman who is capable of bringing new members for the family, so that it can extend and live longer. Thus the woman's body is the private property of her husband. By maintaining and protecting it, there will be no confusion between families in the community. The family, and men in particular, have the responsibility to defend the honor of "their" women.[15]

"A man without honor is a man without religion" is an old Arabic saying that also stresses the intertwined fate of religion and the female body. It implies that achieving honor by being able to control one's female relatives is associated with religion.[16]

There has been little inquiry into where the custom of honor killing comes from in terms of child-rearing practices. That there is widespread sexual abuse of children, and of girls in particular, should be an obvious indicator as to how men in the Arab Muslim world feel about themselves. This behavior undoubtedly contributes to honor killings, which provide a socially accepted outlet, or an escape hatch, for male murderous rage. By acting out through this scapegoat mechanism and by fixating on the female as "the problem" in the family, the clan's males avoid having to behave appropriately. By extension, by mutilating the female body through radical circumcision, the men have identified it concretely as the source of their problem, and it is always ready and available for attack. Estimates show that 80 million women worldwide have experienced genital mutilation. (Female genital mutilation should be called "honor soul murder," since it literally stunts the woman's spirit and vitality and thus murders her female sense of being by preventing orgasm.)

The Arab men's attempt to control women and children is so intense and pervasive that one wonders what else is being covered up. Could honor killings be a social cover-up for incest? In *Sexuality in Islam*, Abdelwahab Bouhdiba specifically stresses that unlike in the Bible, Lot's crime of incest is not mentioned in the foundational narrative of Islam, the Quran.[17] Arab Muslim honor fixates on virginity and sexual purity, which are deemed suspect. Given the documentation of child-rearing practices along with genital mutilation, the question of incest is a legitimate one to pose concerning the male fantasy of female sexual purity, the pervasiveness of abuse, and the practice of restoring honor by murdering females.

Islamic suicide bombings are a form of displaced violence about the Early Mother in life, especially the Early Muslim Mother and the disavowed wish to murder her because she is experienced as engulfing and smothering. Growing up as a devalued girl, the mother has internalized the males' sexism and hatred of the female as self-hatred. Again, my analysis is not intended to blame the mother. If anything, it is to promote more empathy for her and her lack of freedom and to show how her current status impacts the baby she nurtures. The purpose of this book is to point to the urgent need for massive reeducation of these women beginning as early in life as possible.

Domestic violence can result in conjoint murder-suicide. By extension, Islamic suicide terrorism is conjoint group-assisted suicide(s) and mass murder, which enacts a group-held fantasy of hating the "infidel" (Jews, Christians, and at times even Muslim coreligionists). While some readers may find this parallel problematic because I use individual psychology for the group, theirs is a specious argument at best because group processes are grounded in individual processes. A group is constituted through its individuals; moreover, all individuals are formed and born in a state of fusion with the mother. The first group in life is the family.

Just as counterterrorism experts claim that there is no profile for the suicide bomber because there is such diversity in their backgrounds, so too there is diversity among those men and women who murder their family members and commit suicide in domestic violence. A commonality, however, can be found in its act and the group's psychodynamics. We are more alike as humans than we are different. In this regard, suicide terrorism is similar to domestic violence: no culture is immune from it. Domestic violence cuts across all social, economic, political, and religious groups, and it can be premeditated.

There are also commonalities concerning pervasive pathological control, paranoia, and a delusional jealousy heavily tinged with envy because of the inability to separate from the Early Mother. Delusional jealousy is a precursor of homicide in domestic violence.[18] By investigating this difficult and painful terrain, a better understanding of its dynamics might be gained. It may also clarify and promote more empathy for the mothers. Lest we forget, prior to child-bearing age, they were little girls who once were also very vulnerable, devalued, abused, and neglected within their parents' homes and the family clans.

An infant is intimately dependent on its mother at birth and is compelled to fuse with her, not realizing that the mother is a separate person. The Early Mother is only known as "part-object"—the warm breast, the nipple, eyes, mouth, lips, cradling arms, and warm, maternal lap. The infant's desire for fusion is an early, erotic, and physical love that is experienced along with inevitable failures in attunement and causes both pleasure and pain. It is a two-way street as the mother also is fused to the baby out of a need to care for the child as well as its attendant pain and pleasure.

The special name given to this psychological relationship is the "maternal symbiosis" or the "maternal fusion." This twosome, or dyad of mother plus infant, is a merged state that gives life to the baby. The mother is the baby's power supply. Their relationship is a life-giving fusion. The prenatal mother represents the earliest fusional image of the "maternal cameo."

This maternal cameo idea—reminiscent of the image of a mother holding her infant, as in the Madonna and child—gives shape to the psychological concept of maternal fusion. Few of us like to think back to that time when we were completely dependent upon our mothers as helpless infants because it takes us out of our comfort zone. The maternal cameo gives concrete form to the experience of the maternal fusion or symbiosis. The imagery also replicates the terrorist's habit of engaging in concrete, transparent, and imitative behavior because of his or her inability both to separate psychologically from the maternal fusion and to mourn the loss of the Early Mother.

As mentioned above, initially a baby is not aware that the mother is a separate person. Very slowly, as the months pass, the baby gains a growing awareness that Mommy is a whole person. From birth to approximately eighteen months of age, the baby experiences through its senses its mother as a cluster of living body parts: the breast that gives milk, the skin's warmth through touch, the lips that kiss or speak, the eyes that establish visual contact, and the smell of her breast milk and skin. Think now of the all-enveloping burka, which the Taliban has imposed on women in the areas it controls. The burka strips the women of their sensory perceptions and limits the infant's physical contact with its mother. This garment serves one of the objectives in the process of dehumanization.

The developing toddler's integration and representation of the mother as a person in her own right happens over time. Recognizing their mothers as individuals is necessary if little children are going to be able to separate psychologically from their mothers and eventually become persons in their own right with their own center of initiative and assume responsibility for their own actions and thoughts. The goal of this process is becoming an adult.

Suicide terrorism has first arisen in cultures where there is a prohibition against separating from the mother, particularly Arab Muslim and Asian (Japanese, Vietnamese, and Hindu) cultures. These societies are also shame and honor cultures in which the female is devalued and denigrated. Shaming is a means of tying the baby or child to the mother and is a form of pathological control, which is a strategy to fend off being shamed, in turn, and its terrors. It is control through terror—not fear—because it is so early and nonverbal. Yet separating from the mother is all too common a problem in all cultures, including those in the West. There are pockets of shame and honor cultures in the West, such as the culture of sports and the patriarchal, highly traditional family that can be found among all religious dominations.

Children can grow into adulthood having never separated from their mothers in a psychological sense and go through life re-creating the maternal symbiosis by relating to things and others in a concrete way via the maternal cameo, or the image of a loving mother holding and protecting her vulnerable child. We will explore this concept later as it pertains to terrorists who engage the world in a concrete and literal manner.

Could this failure to separate be a clue as to why it is so difficult to explain jihad's intoxicating appeal? None of us ever separate completely from our mothers, but some of us have more difficulties than others do given individual traumatic history. For example, when the Israelis withdrew from the Gaza Strip in the summer of 2005, they were on the lookout for possible Jewish suicide bombers among the settlers whose families are also highly patriarchal. Yet no one could explain the nature of pathological imitative behavior beyond its use as terrorism's tenacious tactical tool or how it arises out of unresolved issues regarding the mother.

Since our discussion concerns Islamic suicide terrorism, it must be noted that of those groups that engage in this form of terrorism, there are more Islam-based terrorist groups than there are terrorist groups associated with any other religion. We need to be honest and directly ask the question why. To beat around the bush is a form of appeasement and demonstrates a terror of confronting aggressive behavior. How can this high frequency rate of Muslim suicide terrorism be explained? To date, the high correlation has not been explained in a satisfactory manner. Considering the psychology of early childhood experience, including shaming practices, in conjunction with the message that a son or daughter is never to separate psychologically from the mother might clarify what causes a child to grow into a terrorist.

In early childhood, eros, or physical desire, is learned at the mother's breast. It forms a template for the infant's later attraction to the other. The infant organizes its emerging self around positive and negative poles with its mother, yielding a love-hate relationship.

In the Arab Muslim world, there is also a long-standing custom of the mother soothing a crying baby boy by stroking his genitals. Such child-rearing practices determine an idiosyncratic sense of pleasure and pain as well as tie the son to his mother more tightly by reinforcing their unbreakable bond both sexually and emotionally. In *Slaughter of the Innocents*, S. J. Breiner noted how common it was in ancient Egypt for wet nurses and nurses to introduce children to sexual activity and "to play and suck on the male child's genitals so that little boys would have stronger erections. This activity was known as 'playing with the sweet finger' or 'little finger.'"[19] Genital manipulation by others continues to this day.[20]

Breiner, citing R. Patai, writes:

> "The mother and grandmother, as well as other female relatives and older siblings will play with the penis of the boy, not only because he is crying but just to make him smile." In Egypt, the mother may attempt to prepare her son gradually for the circumcision operation by "caressing his organ and playfully endeavoring to separate the foreskin from the glans. While doing this she would hum words to the effect that what she is doing will help to make him become a man amongst men."[21]

This interaction goes on until the time of circumcision, which might occur much later in the boy's life. Therefore, he may have many real memories of his mother caressing and fondling his penis for many reasons—not only to caress it but also to clear sand and other debris from under the foreskin—and for many years. The boy is overstimulated, enraged, trapped, and fearful of not being able to control his sexual urges. Allen Edwardes and Robert E. L. Masters also reported how the family may masturbate the infant's penis for hours at a time in order to "increase its size and strengthen it."[22]

Bouhdiba, a French-trained Tunisian psychoanalyst who is also a Muslim, emphasizes the common occurrence of pederasty, mutual masturbation, fellatio, and anal intercourse during childhood in Arab Muslim culture.[23] For example, the word *hammam*, referring to the hot waters of the public bathhouse, is slang for sex because seven- to fourteen-year-old boys go to the baths with their mothers and sisters. Sexuality, eros, and sadism, or gaining power by inflicting pain on the other, even if he is male, are perceived as female attributes. This view of the world is found everywhere but is taboo to discuss, "[even] though it is central in the thinking and the general conversation in the male Arab world." In Bouhdiba's opinion, "Circumcision and excision are like a vaccination against the dangers of sexuality."[24]

There is a lack of awareness that child-rearing practices focusing on the child's genitalia, whether it is a little boy's or a little girl's, mask adult male rage and terror of their feelings of utter impotence. All child-rearing practices revolve around maintaining honor achieved by means of shaming. Since honor is directly linked to the female sex, the genitals of the baby girl are of extreme, if not obsessive, importance. The genitalia determine the baby's status in the hierarchy. It is not surprising then that the genitalia would be altered. Manipulation includes the concrete, physical altering of this particular body part.

Genital mutilation is pervasive throughout the Arab world for both genders. In the Arab world currently there is extensive female genital mutilation, which is subdivided into various types.[25] The first is circumcision, which involves removing the prepuce, or hood of the clitoris. Another version is excision, which involves removing the clitoris and all or parts of the labia minora. The third version is called infibulation, or pharonic circumcision, and is the amputation of the clitoris, the labia minora, and at least the anterior two thirds—and often the entirety—of the labia majora.

A girl child is the recipient of the disavowed rage of her parents as she is the most devalued child. Little girls are to be "protected," that is, made to feel fragile and incompetent in comparison to the boys. It sets them apart as different, meaning bad. The claim is that girls and women cannot control themselves sexually; therefore, their genitalia must be altered by other women but placed under the control of men as they dictate. This command stems from the fantasy that female sexual desire is dangerous and that the female cannot be satiated. According to F. Sabbah, the figure of the female is that of the omnisexual woman.[26] She is the ultimate castrator who overrides the Freudian father, though this idea, too, is a male fantasy imposed on women out of male terror.

Compared to male circumcision, female circumcision is veiled in secrecy. She is attacked because she is considered unclean and dirty. Her life-giving pelvis—that is, her female honor (ird in Arabic)—from which the Arab Muslim is born, is stigmatized as impure.

Even though circumcision for either males or females is not mandated in the Quran itself, the practice is considered to be part of Arab Muslim culture, which perceives the genitals as a sinful body part. While they all feel themselves to be unclean, it is the female baby who pays the price. The female baby is held in such low esteem that she is kept at a developmental disadvantage. She is nursed for a shorter period of time than a male infant is, and she is given less to eat. She is then forced to start working in the family much earlier, at the age of four or five years, than boys are. Little boys are treasured and adored while little girls are despised.

It's not surprising that contempt for females is pervasive and self-perpetuating. Nor is it remarkable that Arab Muslim boys grow up to become men who do not respect women.

In contrast, male circumcision occurs between the ages of two to seven years, but it may occur as late as puberty. It is a celebrated event, with adult males as well as little girls observing it. The celebration is treated like a wedding. In eastern Egypt it is referred to as such—*ars*, meaning "wedding"—with the boy who is to be circumcised called the *khatan*, which means "bridegroom," and the circumcision is the *khitana*.[27] In Morocco the circumcision is considered the boy's first marriage.[28]

The Muslim man may remember the pain and trauma of the circumcision and its extenuating experiences. Those who are able to recall the procedure remember their fear that their penis had actually been cut off and that they were unable to see their penis until the bandages were removed some days later. Only then were they reassured that their penis was still attached. The circumcision is thus experienced as an attack.[29] All those involved deny the trauma of circumcision, but it is terrifying.

A common custom with regard to male circumcision is the infantilizing of the male child by swaddling him after the procedure as if he were a baby: ". . . placed upon his mother's naked back, pressing the bleeding penis until the bandages were removed some days later and were reassured that their penis was still there."[30] The overstimulation mixes the erotic sensation of pleasure with pain, yielding a combustible sadomasochism. The mother as an omnisexual woman is tangibly present at the circumcision. Moroccans believe that the circumcision needs to be remembered by the child and that it should therefore occur at an age when he will not forget the trauma. The circumcision is explicitly linked to *sharaf*, "male honor." As we shall see in chapters 2 and 4, the male circumcision and the suicide bombing are both referred to as a wedding celebration, which is used in order to mark the acquisition of honor.

Another sexual practice involves older males in the clan targeting young boys for anal intercourse, with the latter forced to play out the passive "female" role. This forced subservience does not promote positive identification with women, to say the least. Just as the pain of circumcision is denied, so too is the pain of rape. In ancient Egypt, homosexuality was common in the army. Soldiers believed that they could gain strength by forcing another into being submissive. It was thought that the penetrator would derive more sexual power by dominating his male partner. In turn, such inflicted dominance and experience would make him stronger sexually with women in his future sexual encounters.[31]

However, violence is violence regardless of how we humans label it. Any justification for it can be found after the fact; indeed, practically any religious leader can write a fatwa (legal decree) condoning group-assisted suicide and mass murder but that does not change its psychodynamics. The terror in Islamic suicide terrorism is nothing more than displaced murderous rage meant for the Early Mother, but because of an impaired sense of reality, the terrorists act it out against the Christians (often referred to as the Crusaders), the Jews, and now even against their own Muslim brethren in Saudi Arabia, Iraq, North Africa, Somalia, Afghanistan, and Pakistan, to name only a few countries and regions. The terrorists do so because they have the need to hate and the need to have enemies—needs stemming from the externalization of the hatreds developed through blaming and shaming child-rearing practices, learned in early childhood, while these nascent terrorists were "embedded" in their families.

In contrast to the term "sharaf," some Arabic words for shame, such as *aar*, *khajila*, and *khiziya*, are rarely mentioned in English concerning Arab culture. Could talking about what shame is and how shame causes blame and violence be part of the taboo? For example, to even ask the simple question about where all this shame and humiliation comes from is itself experienced as shaming. This double bind is what makes it nearly impossible for non-Muslims to engage the Arab Muslim world in a discussion about its ongoing lament of being persecuted and its corresponding need to blame the West. But even more important than losing one's honor and being shamed in public is the very *fear* of shame and humiliation, also known as *ayb* (a fear of the fear).

The objective then is to acquire honor by terrifying others into fearing that they will be shamed and humiliated. The matter is further complicated by the fact that honor is a matter of gender and sex so that child-rearing practices revolve around the concrete, physical sex of the child—namely, his or her genitalia.

While in Arab Muslim culture everything is done in order to acquire prestige, which is confused with honor, only male honor, sharaf, can be regained if lost. Men can only regain their honor by willfully spilling blood. Female honor, or ird, which is housed in the pelvis and symbolizes sexual purity, is obsessively guarded and controlled by the male relatives. Once lost or even gossiped about as if the woman or girl had lost her honor, it can never be regained. She is then put to death in an honor killing.

Since every relationship is based on negotiating power, it is easy to see that the relationship between a mother and her infant runs the risk of reproducing the fear of being shamed and humiliated around the issue of genitalia. Because the baby lacks power, he or she is at the complete mercy of the mother, whose ird is under surveillance by male family members, who themselves were once infants. It is an infinite regress. This spiral is the essence of the psychological warfare in the family and clan that a terrified child, especially the little girl, experiences at home.

This unspoken and unexplored war at home contributes to the molding and shaping of Islamic terrorists. While not all abused children become Islamic terrorists, an increasing number are drawn to its violence. The political violence of Islamic suicide terrorism offers the perfect cover to continue to engage in the concrete slaughter of the innocent.

The Islamic suicide terrorists and all their accessories to the crime—the engineer–bomb maker, the recruiter, the sender, the escort, the charismatic leader, their mothers and fathers, their uncles, the clan, the tribe, the umma—

are terrified because they too have been "neotenized." They are all like newborns. They have never been allowed to grow up, to mature, or to be free, independent, self-sufficient, confident, and competent human beings. They have been raised to stay immature all their lives through terrorizing and shaming child-rearing practices. This result also occurs when a family accepts bad behavior as normative, which is common in families where abuse takes place but its members deny it. These individuals then become habituated to death, making it easier for them to join the jihad in general and to volunteer as a suicide bomber in particular. They have been lied to in an insidiously infantilizing, humiliating, and shaming way. They are enraged, and it is estimated 1 percent of the nearly 1.5 billion Muslims become violent jihadis. That is a significant number of jihadis.

In conclusion, as we move on to exploring Arab Muslim culture in light of its specific relationship to the mother, it is important to heed one of the leading Iraqi child psychiatrists, Dr. Sami Timimi:

> In many Arab and Middle Eastern societies traditional child-rearing practices foster behavior orientated towards interdependence rather than individuation and independence. Children are encouraged to express their emotions as opposed to developing self-control over them. By western standards the behaviour of parents towards their children would seem enmeshed and intrusive. Mothers, for example, tend to have a greater interest themselves in their children's affairs. Traditional Arab beliefs view the bond between mother and child as unseverable. The father's role may be seen as more distant but is no less important.[32]

His words underscore the unique nature of the mother-child relationship. The scope of this book elaborates on how that maternal symbiotic tie is the bedrock of the Islamic suicide attack as it is reflected in its graphic imagery. Further, it is uniquely mediated by the ideologies of radical Islam and is supported passive-aggressively by the umma. Hamid calls this kind of behavior passive terrorism.[33]

2

ISLAM: IMITATION OF JUDAISM?

Food for Thought

And when it was said to them, "What is it your Lord sent down?"
They said, "Old folk's tales."
—Sura 16:25

For believers, divine will was made manifest in human discourse when Moses received the law at Mount Sinai.[1] It was the most important moment for Judaism's identity. Like a ladder song, with a new round being added with each verse, Christianity accepted Mosaic law but sought to climb above Judaism by adding the New Testament, which proclaimed Jesus the Messiah. Later, Islam also accepted Mosaic law as well as the New Testament with Jesus represented as a prophet of Islam and a precursor of Muhammad's. Islam then added the prophecy of Muhammad, yielding the Quran.[2] Moses is the person mentioned most often in the Quran. Islam tried to claim the truth over Christianity and Judaism by reopening revelations with the "Prophet of the Seal" as Muhammad is called. Moses' law initiates the particular shaping of each respective group's sacred scriptures: the Hebrew Torah, the Christian New Testament, and the Muslim Quran. Psychoanalytically, each scripture serves as a distinct self-object for the group self of the faith community.

Islam is chronologically the last of the revelations, even though Muslims believe that the Quran existed prior to the Torah and the New Testament and that the Jews and Christians perverted the message of Allah. The Prophet Muhammad found himself in the position of having to up the ante with regard to ideologies. After borrowing from the preexisting Torah and New Testament, he then had to distance Islam from them by creating a different religious identity.

To cite only one example, the concept of martyrdom exists in all three religions, but the imagery in each is different. For the Jew, the precept of *Kiddush haShem* (sanctification of the name of God) dictates the following action: if someone says, "Kill A or I'll kill you," you are not permitted to kill A because your blood "is . . . [not] redder than his." Therefore, you must allow yourself to be killed rather than kill another. This precept, however, does not mean that you should take your own life.[3] In Christianity, both Jesus Christ on the cross dying for his followers' sins and Joan of Arc being burned at the stake for adhering to her beliefs are the essence of martyrdom. This form of martyrdom does not involve a death fusion, that is, conjoint murder-suicide. But in Islam, it is well known that the *shahid* (martyr) is a person who commits both suicide and murder at the same time. Here, the escalation of violent deaths is quite different.

By looking at the patriarchs held sacred to all three religions, we can learn more about the definition of religious group as terrorist group by alterity, or otherness. Besides Moses, Abraham is also a figure of authority in all three religions. While Jews, Christians, and Muslims are referred to as "the children of Abraham,"[4] Jews and Christians have often viewed themselves as the "parents" of Islam.[5] Recently, Akbar S. Ahmed relates, a Jewish chaplain used the concept of "three sisters" for the three Abrahamic faiths: sometimes they quarrel, other times they are friends, but nonetheless they all belong to the same family.[6] Each has an ongoing relationship in real time with the other two.

While Sigmund Freud described authority as paternal or Oedipal, contemporary psychoanalysts understand that often the father is a stand-in for the Early Mother because the infant's first power struggle in life is with its mother.[7] Man created religion in order to fill a painful void left by the inability to mourn the loss of the Early Mother.[8] S. G. Shoham put it well in the title of his book

God as the Shadow of Man: Myth and Creation.[9] While Judaism is accepted by Christianity as temporally the first Abrahamic faith, Islam rejects this position through the belief (*fitra* in Arabic) that Abraham was never a Jew in Sura 3:67. Islam's goal is to usurp Abraham's authority and thereby claim the ultimate authority. This aim is understandable given the hurt that Muhammad must have experienced when the Jews of Medina did not accept him as a prophet. However, this fitra cannot hide the fact that in historical time as opposed to religious or mythic time, Judaism occurred and developed first.

Could being "first" be the fundamental psychoanalytic reason why Judaism and the Jews are so hated and why anti-Semitism is so pervasive and persistent? Judaism may be identified unconsciously with the Early Mother. At times Judaism is venerated and at times reviled. This dissociated love-hate relationship is called splitting, which also occurs with the Early Mother because she is the first person the infant experiences intimately in both blissful eros and miserable terror. The Early Mother embodies the conflicting senses of at-targhib (enticing) and at-tarhib (scaring).

The Early Mother is the first other. Underlying the idea of "first" is the concept of "one." The ordinal equivalent of counting forward from one is first, second, third, fourth, and so on. Thus, the position of first and the number one are inextricably linked semantically in the unconscious.

This connection is of no small consequence when considering that the idea of monotheism (in the Greek, *monos* means "alone" or "singular") is also grounded in the notion of oneness, that is, one God. Oneness is also the essence of the maternal symbiosis. Psychoanalytically, monotheism's obsessive preoccupation with one god is signaled in a reference to the unity represented by the maternal symbiosis of mother and infant. An image held sacred by Christianity and Islam (even though the latter forbids graven images) is that of the Virgin Mary with the baby Jesus. As we have seen in chapter 1, this maternal cameo graphically represents the idea that the psychological birth of the infant equals the maternal symbiosis.

It is not within the scope of this chapter either to examine the Abrahamic familial relations in depth or to explore how Judaism has borrowed from

Islam, especially from the seventh century to the fifteenth century. Suffice it to say regarding the latter, Judaism heavily borrowed poetic, grammatical, and literary forms; some scientific learning; architecture; and even women's head coverings from Islam. Jewish scholars frequently acknowledge such borrowing. In addition, Jews and Muslims often intermarried, especially during the eighth century, resulting in mutual borrowing. As Avner Falk notes, "Many present-day Israeli Jews who came from Muslim countries resemble the Muslims of their countries of origin in looks, speech, food, and habits more than they do their fellow Jews from Western countries."[10] My remarks are limited to exploring the relevance and implication of the assertion that Islam is an "imitation" of Judaism—an assertion made by Thomas Patrick Hughes and Sigmund Freud—and why the tendency to speak of the Abrahamic family may be inflaming the current situation regarding anti-Semitism and Islamic suicide terrorism.

In *A Dictionary of Islam*, first published in 1885 in London, Hughes wrote:

> Many of the doctrines and social precepts of the Qur'an are also from Judaism. . . . Whilst, therefore, Muhammad took little of his religious system from Christianity, he was vastly indebted to Judaism both for his historical narratives and his doctrines and precepts. Islam is nothing more nor less than Judaism plus the Apostleship of Muhammad. The teachings of Jesus form no part of his religious system.[11]

Hughes spent twenty years as a Christian missionary in Peshawar, Pakistan, composing the dictionary for scholars of comparative religion, British colonial administrators, and travelers. He disingenuously claims it was not meant as a weapon against Islam. Furthermore, Hughes misleads the reader by claiming that Jesus plays no important role in Islam. He contradicts himself, because not only is the Quran replete with verses about Jesus but his own dictionary cites them. His curious comment signals his own unconscious distancing from both of the Semitic peoples and their scriptures, with Christianity coming out on top! Hughes's dictionary is still in print to this day and remains a critical reference for many scholars.

In "Moses and Monotheism," Freud wrote: "The founding of the Mahommedan religion seems to me like an abbreviated repetition of the Jewish one, of which it emerged *as an imitation* [emphasis added]."[12] This reference to Islam is a hapax legomenon, the only time that Islam is ever mentioned in all of Freud's scientific writings. It is curious, too, because Islam's jihad had reached the gates of Vienna in 1683. Oriental rugs graced Freud's consulting room as well as the fainting couch. His article featured multiple identifications with the "Orient" and with being Jewish and Semitic. Yet, lost in James Strachey's sanitized translation is not just a specific gesture to both Luther and Erasmus,[13] but also Freud's use of *Nachahmung* connotes a counterfeit or bad imitation.[14]

Was Freud anxious when he wrote this essay? Did he displace his mounting fears? On the preceding page, Freud had pondered the haunting eternal question as to why the Jews, his people, are so hated. His reply is simple: they were the "firstborn" of God.[15] Is it possible that Freud dreaded the maternal presence lurking behind the chosen son theme? It is well accepted that Freud could not and did not elaborate a theory for the Early Mother in his writings because of his conflicted, ambivalent relationship with his own mother. His mother called him *mein goldener* (my golden) Sigi, and she made it known that he was her favorite son. Nonetheless, Freud's anxieties about Islam were, in part, reality based because in his time the Grand Mufti Haj Amin al-Husseini (Muslim jurist) of Jerusalem was busy forming an alliance with the Nazis.[16] In turn, they were breathing down Freud's neck in Vienna while he labored over this article's very manuscript. Ultimately he was forced to flee to England for his life. Four of his sisters—Dolfi, Mitzi, Rosa, and Pauli—were not as fortunate and were murdered in Nazi concentration camps.

Freud's strikingly similar accusations of Islam being an imitative religion raise the issue of whether he had access to Hughes's dictionary. A cursory review of his library does not confirm an instance of source influence.[17] It does not rule out the possibility, however, that he unconsciously drew upon a nineteenth-century Orientalist stereotype of Islam or that he may have been acquainted with Abraham Geiger's 1832 essay "Was hat Mohammed aus dem Judenthume aufgenommen? (What Has Mohammed Taken [or Borrowed] from Judaism?)"

What is also so startling is that during this same time frame, H. Deutsche, one of Freud's disciples, described the "as-if" personality type, which she deemed imitative.[18] The designation describes an individual who has a weak sense of self though he or she creates a convincing illusion of having a solid identity, but that identity masks a pathological dependency on others in order to facilitate a temporary persona of knowing what to do and how to be moment-to-moment. Thus, the tendency to imitate is pervasive and at first not noticeable. The word "imitation" in this discussion can take on a pejorative meaning. Imitation can also be the denial of enmeshment and fusion. What exactly is fusion for identity? I have noted that the suicide attack is a death fusion—that is, a merger with an idealized other to fend off the fear and terror of one's own sense of self as well as a denial on the part of the person seeking the merger as a defense against recognizing one's own omnipotence and grandiosity. Merging, or fusion, has its own eros, and in its most concrete form, it finds expression in sex, which also raises the issue of gender for the sense of self.

One particular dimension of fusion needs to be explored here. In its most explicit occurrence, the case of erotomania-motivated murder may be informative for the violence between Judaism and Islam as enunciated by those Islamists who feel they must annihilate all Jews.

In erotomania-related killing, the murder is motivated by an offender-victim relationship that is based on the offender's fixation. This fantasy commonly is expressed in such forms as fusion (the offender blends his personality into the victim's) or erotomania (a fantasy based on idealized romantic love or spiritual union of a person [rather than sexual attraction]). This preoccupation with the victim becomes consuming and ultimately leads to the victim's death. The drive to kill arises from a variety of motives, ranging from rebuffed advances to internal conflicts stemming from the offender's fusion of identity with the victim.

The distinguishing characteristic of this type of murder is found in the victimology. The victim targeted is very often a person with high mass media visibility of local, national, or international scope. Through this exposure, the victim comes to the attention of the offender.[19] [The reader might think here about Judaism, Jews, and Israel as always being in the news.]

The victim is almost always perceived as someone of higher status. When erotomania is involved, the victim (usually someone unattainable to the offender) becomes the imagined lover of the offender through hidden messages known only to the offender. The offender builds an elaborate fantasy revolving around this imagined love. Male erotomaniacs tend to act out this fantasy with greater force. When this acting out is rebuffed, the erotomaniac decides to guarantee that no one else will steal his or her imagined lover. If this idealized person will not belong to him, then the offender ensures that the victim will not be given the chance to belong to anyone.[20]

It is possible to entertain this idea in light of Islam's wish for all Jews to revert to Islam (since according to Islam every person is born Muslim) and leave their Jewish identity behind. In light of the political domestic violence discussion, Judaism would be the "imagined lover." Perhaps this scenario reflects the case of the radical political Islamist who must murder in comparison to a Muslim who does not have the need to hate or have enemies.

Imitation becomes frightening when it moves into a fusional state with the other. Take, for example, Mark David Chapman's murder of John Lennon. It is a classic case of male erotomania-motivated killing, a psychiatric condition mixed with psychosexual dynamics predicated on an obsession with a celebrity as a way of consolidating a fragile sense of self. Chapman began to imitate Lennon's life. Further, "Chapman had apparently been building a fantasy life centered on John Lennon for several years. He married a wife of Japanese descent in an attempt to mimic Lennon's Japanese wife. He collected Beatles albums and played in a rock band. Chapman decided to retire from music at the age of twenty-five because Lennon also had been in retirement."[21]

An explanation for Chapman's motive may be found in a psychiatrist's testimony during his trial: "The more Chapman imitated Lennon, the more he came to believe he was John Lennon. He eventually began to look upon Lennon as a phony. The fusion of his identity with Lennon became so engulf-ing that Chapman decided he, too would become a phony if he didn't stop the process in Lennon."[22]

The crux of imitation becomes problematic if and when the fusion of identity becomes excessive, that is, obsessional and fixated. The idealized other who is initially venerated and placed on a pedestal is quickly de-idealized and attacked. In the worst-case scenario, the other is murdered when the imita-tor or offender "feels his own identity is threatened by the existence of the person he has patterned his life after or when the offender feels the person he has imitated no longer lives up to the offender's ideal."[23] The reader might consider that because the Islamists are threatened both by the freedom in the democratic state of Israel and by the Jews' ability to enjoy life, Islamists such as Osama bin Laden see Judaism as no longer living up to the ideals of the Torah, which the Prophet Muhammad embraced in the Quran when Judaism was perceived as good and pure. Hence, the Jews, Judaism, and Islam's Judaic roots must be eliminated by jihad. It is as though Islam is an "as-if" religion. As in a legal case, the evidence that the Jews came first needs to be destroyed. But is this discussion of Islam being an imitation of Judaism defensive on Freud's and Hughes's parts, who represent Judaism and Christianity by proxy? Is it not a means by which Freud and Hughes could dismiss the need to have to deal with the reality of Islam in a mature manner? Is it also a way of relegating Islam to the realm of fantasy through denial? Would it not also be offensive to Muslims? Such stereotyping neither promotes peaceful coexistence nor deters violence.

Perhaps Judaism and Jews have not been able to deal with their pain of watching the Holy Torah being tampered with and taken over by Islam as Muhammad "amended" it with his further revelations. Could it be that even today Jews continue to feel shadowed by Islam because of their irrational fears and unarticulated fantasies that Islam will steal even more of their identity?

Such unidentified fantasies may have inadvertently caused Judaism and Jews to cling to the idea of "chosen-ness," which can easily become confused with the grandiosity of being special. Poorly understood even among Jews, chosen-ness or "elected-ness" is not supposed to be an exclusionary doctrine. Anyone can convert to Judaism should he or she desire to do so, provided the person studies and accepts the Covenant.

Could Judaism inadvertently be pouring oil on Islamic flames of rage by inferring that it is a counterfeit imitation? By not consciously knowing its terror and dread of being overwhelmed and engulfed by Islam, Judaism resides in a psychohistorical blind spot. However, all terror is in part reality based. The terrors of Judaism's followers become clearer when one considers world demographics of religious adherents. There are approximately 1.2 billion Muslims in comparison to 12 million–14 million Jews, or a ratio of about 1,000 to 1.[24] The disparity in numbers suggests the Jews' engulfment.

Imitation or copying can also imply the existence of a double, or almost a twin. Having a double helps and hinders. On the one hand, it protects the self from isolation and loneliness.[25] On the other, the double can be split off, projected on to the other, and then attacked. A person or a group never has to learn how to contain aggression and rage because the former can simply blame and attack the other. Could this situation be the case for Judaism and Islam? Could their adherents have had a long-standing, ambivalent, and bloody relationship (as well as some moments of peaceful coexistence, for example, in medieval Spain and the Ottoman Empire) because they are so close in sacred Semitic languages, customs, law, and geography? They are nearly doubles in some key respects.

Islam is not without its problems, which may be detected in its globalizing tendency to lay claim to everything and everyone from the moment of creation as it asserts its legitimacy and declares it is the first of the monotheisms. To offer a recent example of this propensity, Ahmed relates that he was teaching his college students about Islam's inclusiveness and coexistence concerning the three Abrahamic faiths and brought in a famous Saudi scholar to talk with his class. The scholar proclaimed to them, "I am a Jew, I am a Christian, and I am a Muslim," citing the reason being that Islam accepts the religious legacy of Judaism and Christianity.[26] However, could not this assertion be experienced as offensive to a Jew as if this Muslim scholar is determining the identity of Judaism for Jews? Along with this claim another important Islamic ideology, which buttresses this globalizing tendency, is the belief that Abraham was not a Jew (Sura 3:60). Another retrospective belief is that Allah created Islam at the beginning of time, and Adam was the first Muslim. Yet a third claims that every human being is born a Muslim, and only parental ignorance leads the child away from the true religion, Islam. Even the Islamic creation of *dhimmeh*, the protection offered to People of the Book, is patronizing.[27] Ironically, these beliefs begin to show how Islam differs from Judaism.

The idea of imitation itself is part of the source-influence conundrum; under other conditions, imitation is said to be the highest form of flattery. Borrowing goes on all the time, yet no group owns a language or even has exclusive rights to sacred writings.

In an example of borrowing, each pillar of the Five Pillars of Islam can be traced back to Judaism:

> the Arabic *Shahada*, the bearing of witness to the oneness of God and the prophethood of Muhammad, and the Hebrew *Shm'a*, affirmation of faith in one God;
>
> *Salat* (Arabic), prayer five times a day (though it is also thought to have been influenced by Zoroastrianism), and *Tefila* (Hebrew), prayer three times a day;
>
> *Tsawm* (Arabic), fasting from dawn to dusk during the month of Ramadan, and *Tsom* (Hebrew), fasting generally from sunset to sundown (both deriving from the same proto-Semitic root);
>
> *Sadaka* (Arabic), the giving of alms or charity, and *Tsedaka* (Hebrew), the giving of alms (again the Arabic and Hebrew terms are cognates); and
>
> *Haj* (Arabic), the pilgrimage to Mecca, and *Aliyah* (Hebrew), or "going

up"—that is, the pilgrimage to Jerusalem three times a year as cited in the Bible.

Could Islam's unacknowledged indebtedness to Judaism be another part of the problem? Debt is a reminder of maternal dependency.[28] Are Jews asking too much of Islam and Muslims to recognize their Judaic roots? Allow me to extend the metaphor of the mother-son relationship for the sake of argument. Should the Judaic mother demand of her Muslim son such gratitude? Gratitude can never be coerced, however; it must be given of one's own volition. Cast in the role of Early Mother but blind to it, Judaism and Jews may be looking for recognition in all the wrong places.

By way of conclusion, one recent development might be food for thought—that is, the commonality of Jewish and Islamic dietary laws known respectively as *kashrut* (Hebrew for allowed, or kosher) and *halal* (Arabic for lawful). At a growing number of American colleges, such as Mount Holyoke and Dartmouth, an effort has emerged to meet the dietary needs of Jewish and Muslim students by providing kosher and halal food services. While Middle East politics may be too sensitive an issue to discuss at the dinner table, Jewish and Muslim students are sharing some of the same food, though reciting different blessings over it according to their respective traditions. Sitting together, they make manifest the etymological meaning of companion (literally, *com-*, or "with," and *panis*, or "bread"), or breaking bread together. Explicitly maternal, dietary laws articulate a safe frame around food that nurtures. Whoever sits at the dinner table should always be counted as a full-fledged member in a family. The fact that Islamic law allows Muslims to eat kashrut as halal is also an unconscious gesture recognizing its Jewish "mother."

However, for Jews, halal does not equate with kashrut. It is a reminder of their differences and that the metaphor of familial relations has its limitations. In reality, Judaism is not Islam's mother, and Islam is not Judaism's son. When the November 9, 2005, suicide bombings occurred in Amman, Jordan, a front-page article appeared in the Saturday edition of the *New York Times* with the headline "Many in Jordan See Old Enemy in Attack: Israel." The article captured the following sentiment: "While most Arabs have long viewed Israel as their enemy, the extent to which Israel weighs on the regional psyche and diverts attention away from social, political, religious and economic issues cannot be ignored, many social and political analysts say. Blaming Israel is not just a knee jerk, they say; for many Arabs, it is their reality."[29]

As relationship metaphors, though, they create and shape powerful unconscious wishes and fantasies in the psychodynamics of the Abrahamic family. By force of fantasy, if unaware, the violence surrounding the fantasy is acted out inappropriately with others, as is the case of Islamic suicide terrorism against the Jews and the Crusaders. In the end, Judaism and Islam are religious systems tied to cultures, languages, and geography that are very similar but also different. Therefore, they should not fear and dread each other the way that they do.

It is when Jews and Muslims attempt to work out their respective unconscious issues with their own "parents" in the public arena of interreligious warfare that they have problems. By recognizing and containing one's own feelings of shame, humiliation, and rage, rather than experiencing these internal persecutory feelings as veridical and equal to external reality, then there exists the real possibility to avoid war. War is the misrecognition of the other as feared when, in fact, the other is familiar and legitimate. The language of metaphor locks in projective identifications about family issues that belong in their respective families, but, even more important, the feelings of rage need to be contained within the self and not projected even on to one's own family members.[30] Admittedly, heeding this advice is a tall order. However, pondering the dilemma may clear the ground to identify more islands of coexistence from which to build a more viable peace in a realistic way rather than persisting in clinging to overidealized notions of family, as in that of Abraham's.

3

THE DEATH PILOTS OF
SEPTEMBER 11

Heaven lies beneath the feet of the mother.
—Arabic saying

In chapter 1, I suggested political domestic violence as a psychoanalytic theory. Briefly, the theory involves the Early Mother. Since the Early Mother is the first intense relationship in life for the infant, the relationship becomes the space in which the infant experiences the terror of abandonment as well as bliss because he or she is completely dependent upon his or her mother. Splitting of the bad parts of the infant's perceptions must be projected on to the Early Mother, making her the "bad" Early Mother, and develops into paranoid rage. In order to heal the infantile pain and frustration, the infant seeks to recapture blissful moments with the "good" Early Mother. This process has been called the beginnings of the psychological birth of the infant—namely, the maternal symbiosis or maternal fusion. Where there has been chronic, pervasive deprivation and misattunement, along with intergenerational transmission of trauma, genetics, and even biochemistry, we might speculate that the deck of cards is stacked against the infant and that the infant is at risk of growing into a terrorist. But in the case of Islamic suicidal terrorism as well as domestic violence, an added element of severity leads the terrorized individual into act-ing out this rage against the Early Mother by seeking to kill her off—that is, murdering her—as well as by committing suicide, which is self-murder.

The nineteen hijackers of September 11, 2001, sought a fusion in death with the Early Mother through conjoint suicide and murder with a twist—sa-cred suicide of a subgroup of a terrorist organization and mass murder. To gain a better understanding of the death fusion and the psychodynamics involved, four of the main hijackers will be discussed: Hani Hanjour, Mohammed Atta, Marwan Al-Sheyhi, and Ziad Samir Jarrah.

In an MSNBC television documentary, Forrest Sawyer, an accomplished journalist, called these hijackers the Death Pilots.

Three copilots operated under Atta: Abdulaziz al-Omari and the Al-Shehri brothers—twenty-one-year-old Waled and twenty-five-year-old Wail, who was known to be suffering from chronic depression.[1] As bizarre as this description may sound, these Arab fanatics actually fell in love with America, even though in the end they sought to murder her. This perverse love affair re-sulted in a "murderous wedding dance" ending in a death of fusion. The Tuni-sian psychoanalyst Abdelwahab Bouhdiba noted that Muslims love to marry,[2] but he failed to mention this particular kind of marriage, which is called *Ars al-Shahada*, or the "martyr's marriage."

A suicide murderer's personality does not arise de novo; rather, it is shaped very early by his or her first relationship in life, that with the mother. This interaction is where an infant experiences primary feelings of total terror and blissful eros, but the key concept is power, which is confused with path-ological control. The significant image is a dyad: either person plus person, person plus a fused group, or person plus an inanimate object. For example, mother plus baby would be the most common and fundamental dyad. The famous sacred dyad for Christianity is the Virgin Mary plus Baby Jesus. This dyad is also held sacred in Islam as Muhammad recognized the New Testa-ment, even though graven images are not permitted.[3] Nonetheless, since Islam embraces the New Testament along with its images, it cannot expunge from its cultural memory the received images of Christianity, which include the Madonna and child, so central to its theosophy. Yet for radical political Islam, this image poses a dilemma because Christianity is the Islamists' reviled enemy. They must hate but still unconsciously love the sacred image of mother and child, and they must obsessively seek it in a concrete manner to destroy it because the image cannot be controlled.

In the psychoanalytic literature to date, no term complements and graphically represents the maternal symbiosis of life's first dyad. For many who suffer pathological issues of individuation and separation, the maternal symbiosis may take on a concrete dimension as attempts at mastering the terrors surrounding individuation and separation recycle, but cognitively it cannot be processed and understood; it is where insight is not enough. Such was the case for the Death Pilots.

The Death Pilots' inability to think metaphorically made them concretely experience the world and act out their rage. The Death Pilots mistook their fantasy thoughts to be reality. They translated their fantasies by acting them out in real time. Their fantasies of rage against their mothers because of their unhealthy "mama's boy" dependency propelled them forward into fusing with their mothers in death, but the infidels were their maternal replacement. So we see then that the underlying fusion of the maternal cameo is buried within the imagery of death and destruction.

Some important maternal cameos bespeak death, sacrifice, and heroism. It has been noted that perhaps the most famous image seared into our minds from the Oklahoma City bombing of the Alfred P. Murrah Federal Building on April 19, 1995, was that of the fireman carrying the bloodied baby. It is reminiscent of Michelangelo's *Pietà*, the sculpture of Mary holding the lifeless body of her son Jesus. For Islam, perhaps the most sacred maternal cameo is encountered at the moment of death for the Prophet Muhammad, who is said to have died with his head on the breast of his wife Aisha as she cradled him in her lap.[4] Of his nine to fourteen purported wives, Aisha was the most special because she was the only wife who was a virgin at the time of their marriage—when she was only seven years old. "From womb to tomb," Muhammad was buried in her room where she continued to live. The burial site set the precedence for a martyr's death: they are buried where they fall, thus obviating the ritual washing.[5]

Thus inscribed into the maternal cameo for Islam is sacrifice and death with a hint of necrophilia.[6] The Death Pilots of September 11, 2001, also engaged in such pervasive magical thinking. They believed they could change the world to conform to their own thoughts. It is a common hallmark of all Islamic suicidal terrorists and their radical political groups.

In cultures as well as with individuals, magical thinking predominates where and when there is a great deal of shame and humiliation. It is the force of omnipotence and grandiosity because it is left over from childhood and represents the child's distinct way of making sense of the world. Magical thinking serves as a protective defense against dealing maturely with the pain of one's shame. It facilitates splitting at an unconscious level and helps to maintain it by providing an opportunity to project one's bad parts and feelings on to others and then to attack them.

Bernard Lewis, the eminent scholar of Arab and Muslim society and history, put it well in addressing the question, why do they hate us (that is, the West)? He contends it is the wrong question to ask. He points out, "You can't be rich, strong, successful and loved, particularly by those who are not rich, not strong and not successful. So the hatred is something almost axiomatic. The question which we should be asking is why do they, the Arab Muslim world, neither fear nor respect us?"[7] The answer can be found in the sense of grandiosity that is a response to deep-seated fear, disavowed and denied, that promotes no limits or boundaries and hence no respect.

While much of the Arab world calls the suicide murderer a *shahid*, or martyr, and the victim a *kafir* (infidel), these labels are nothing more than a paranoid manipulation of the religious code that cleverly defends against infantile self-hatred by projecting it on to its murder victims. The suicide murderer Death Pilot, for example, was on a final mission for one last connection with his mother, albeit perversely. His world was one of splitting the idealized good Early Mother from the bad Early Mother.

By examining the Death Pilots' relationships in terms of the schizoid character type, a deeper understanding of their motivations may result. The schizoid is the underbelly of paranoia.[8] The term has not received much attention with regard to the suicide bombers. I use schizoid as a descriptor rather than as a diagnostic label. While it is not my aim to make a clinical diagnosis, which is impossible, the language of the clinic nonetheless provides a different way to conceptualize suicidal terrorism. The term "schizoid" is used clinically to describe such characteristics as distancing from, avoiding, and orbiting around people rather than relating to them directly and as feeling safer with hard objects that can be manipulated and serve as substitutes for real relationships.[9] Schizoid also signals annihilating rage as in the question of the jihadis' behavior. In the working paper, "Engineers of Jihad," Diego Gambetta and Steffen Hertog raise the question of schizoid behavior and perhaps even autism as warranting further investigation.[10] Indeed, the bomb maker of jihad is called 'muhandis (engineer). In the fall of 2008 Professor Norman Simms and I authored an essay on this subject, "Jihaditism? Parallels between Autism and Terrorism."[11] Much work needs to be done on the way in which terrorists bond with their objects.

Flying provides a good window into the schizoid dilemma with man's grandiose and omnipotent wishes.[12] The term "schizoid dilemma" was first used to describe patients who suffered from a pervasive sense of futility because they felt the threat of the loss of the object, meaning of the early maternal connection as well as of the self.[13] They felt completely impotent. Recently the concept was postmodernized and applied cleverly to the schizoid dilemma of punk rockers.[14] Pilots, meanwhile, love being in control by being at the controls. The maternal cameo in this scenario is the pilot plus the plane. In the cockpit, the pilot is at one with his instruments and is plugged into his "motherboard." While few pilots turn into Death Pilots and take up suicidal murder, those who have been hooked into a fused group by a charismatic leader are more prone to carry out such destructive wishes. Even though the Death Pilots were taking orders from "headquarters" (as if they did not become pilots by their own volition and were on "autopilot"), the entire mission must have resonated with their own unconscious destructive wishes. They were simultaneously macho pilots and scapegoats who were sacrificed by their larger group. They were therefore perceived as expendable, just as women are, and thus as expressing the drive to become both sexes because they also felt utterly emasculated.[15] Anat Berko refers to the suicide bomber as both victimizer and victim.

Furthermore, a colleague once described the airplane as an interesting schizoid object choice for the maternal fusion for it is hard on the outside and womblike on the inside. Upon takeoff, the Death Pilot is fused with the good Early Mother. When the mother ship levels off at a cruising altitude, this fusion deepens. The pilot begins to fear engulfment. A paranoid shift ensues whereby what is familiar becomes unfamiliar and scary, if not terrifying. Freud called this *Das Unheimlich*, "the uncanny."[16] The mother ship morphs into a phallic missile of mass destruction, targeting its victims, plowing into and destroying Mother Earth or the Twin Towers, and ending in a death fusion.[17]

Hani Hanjour was twenty-nine years old when he flew into the Pentagon.[18] He grew up in a Saudi mountain resort town where his father was a food supplier. Hanjour was described as extremely shy, withdrawn, short, slight, and not very masculine. His eldest brother by eleven years, Aburrahman, acted as a surrogate father and treated him in an infantile way. During his second trip to America, Hanjour, then twenty-six years old, was still regarded as unable to take care of himself and needing a chaperone (as a Muslim girl would). Aburrahman arranged for Hanjour to stay with friends of his, a married couple living in Florida. They later described Hanjour as having incredibly poor hygiene, right down to the green film on his teeth, which he hadn't brushed in weeks. Poor hygiene is a red flag for mental health, and unbrushed teeth hint at disavowed oral rage. After his stint in Florida, Hanjour moved to Arizona, where he barely managed to learn to fly by keeping at it in a pressuring way—the hallmark of a controlling, passive-aggressive person who can't take no for an answer. Once in the flight simulator, its instruments would immediately overwhelm him. Unlike the good schizoid who easily finds his way with hard, inanimate objects because he feels more secure with them than with people, Hanjour seemed to be caught in limbo between the animate and the inanimate. Up to the very end, Hanjour was still trying to learn how to fly.

Instructors at his last school in the Washington, D.C., area decided that he was so bad that they would not allow him to rent a plane. Yet as more information was obtained about Hanjour, it is now believed that it was just a deceptive ploy on his part to play dumb, and, in fact, he was an excellent pilot.

Meek, introverted, and smelly, Hanjour's untethered personality fit Al-Qaeda's target recruitment of unsophisticated young men to be used as expendable helpers. They were known as "mules" by operatives.

Yet, Hanjour was not a mule.[19] According to a seasoned airline pilot who reviewed the four planes and their routes of terror, Hanjour had the hardest task of all—to crash on descent into his target, which requires much more skill than driving a plane horizontally into buildings such as the Twin Towers.[20] In retrospect, closed-source corroboration—meaning those who work in intelligence with special access to closed sources—confirms that Hanjour was anything but a nerd. He was highly sophisticated and handpicked for the job. He was able to present himself as incompetent to others and yet hide the fact that he knew how to fly planes. As for his green film–covered teeth, it is possible that he could have regressed while in the home of his brother's friends who were to act as his adopted family. He could have really wanted them to take care of him and unknowingly have presented himself in such a needy way that he actually failed to care for himself. His fear could have been manifest through such nonverbal cues. This behavior would have been a kind of splitting.

Bin Laden's ringleader for the Death Pilots of September 11, Mohammed Atta, is a stark contrast to Hanjour. Everyone remembers the thirty-three-year-old Atta as a vividly arrogant, boorish, stingy, and hot-tempered man who hated women and Jews.[21] He often exhibited out-of-control behavior, such as binge drinking, and had a favorite Hamburg prostitute whom he liked to beat up in order to satisfy himself sexually.[22] Indeed, his father, Mohammad al-Amir Atta, described him in the following, revealing way: "My son is a very sensitive man; he is soft and was *extremely attached to his mother* [emphasis added]. I almost tricked him to go to Germany to continue his education. Otherwise, he never wanted to leave Egypt." Amir continued, "He didn't want to go."[23] Atta clearly had separation issues, and at one point he wanted to return to his mother. "Just before coming to Kandahar, he [Atta] asked his mother if he could move back to Egypt to care for her. It was almost as if he were asking someone else to stop him from something he knew he couldn't stop himself from doing."[24] His violence against women did not occur in a vacuum, apart and separate from the political violence he perpetrated against Christian America in the destruction of the World Trade Center. They are indeed related.

Atta exemplifies the perpetrator who cannot contain his murderous rage as it spills outward. Forrest Sawyer's 2002 interview of Atta's father revealed a furious, paranoid Egyptian lawyer whom Atta could never please. Amir blatantly ascribed to the routine Arab conspiracy theory that it was the Israelis who attacked the World Trade Center. Amir is a control freak, and it is little wonder that Atta would be his mirror image. Nowhere in the psychoanalytic literature has the subject of pathological control been explicitly linked to paranoia, even though it lies at the heart of the behavior and is a concrete manifestation of the pathology of enactments. In a recent work, Aubrey Immelman applied the concept of the puritanical compulsive character to Atta, stressing this very issue.[25] Immelman also noted a behavior of Atta's: until he went to college, he liked to sit in his mother's lap, just as if he were a little boy who craved her warmth, love, and protection. Clearly this maternal cameo speaks volumes as mother and son flaunted their exclusive fusion in front of their husband and father, respectively, in a concrete manner.

Atta's regression, seeking the sensuous and voluptuous Early Mother, also fostered a delusion that was confirmed by his last will, in which he forbade pregnant women from attending his funeral. "I don't want a pregnant woman or a person who is not clean to come and say good-bye to me because I don't approve it."[26] Such intense gender apartheid indicates phobia, whose underlying mechanisms are also schizoid, as Hannah Segal noted.[27]

The Muslim terrorists are sexually insecure. It should not come as a surprise that they use child pornography to obtain perverse pleasure. Quoting Anwar Hekmat, an expert on the Quran: "The prevailing opinion among orthodox Muslim men seems to be that men and women are like fire and gunpowder: in close proximity they're liable to explode from unchecked sexual desire. They should therefore be kept as far apart as possible (through both veiling and seclusion) to reduce the potential for social evils."[28] Islamic suicide terrorism thus becomes the socially sanctioned outlet for a concrete explosion of such repressed sexual desire.

The obsession for purity, which dreads the female body while also craving it, is a recurrent theme in political Islam. Atta also fixated on rescuing his Islamic *madina*, Cairo, from Westernization. Meaning "city" in Arabic and having a feminine gender, madina provides the variant for Medina, the name of the second holiest city for Islam. (It comes after Mecca and before Jerusalem.) Falk notes that Jerusalem, and cities in general, often represent the idealized archaic Early Mother.[29] Howard Stein, a leader in the field of psychogeography, has repeatedly stressed the significance of space and place in the unconscious of an individual; it is often linked to the mother's body.[30] In Atta's psycho-geography, skyscrapers poisoned the idealized maternal fusion and mocked the holy minaret.

Jason Burke writes that "the concepts of space, and more particularly, the idea of 'Islamicized space' are hugely important to many militant Islamic activists and repeatedly feature in their literature and discourse."[31] Moreover, by following Atta's disturbed and delusional line of thought, it is important to note that the first tower to be attacked was the North Tower of the World Trade Center. The North Tower stood six feet taller than the South Tower and of the two buildings had the huge antennae. Like Seattle's Space Needle, which Al-Qaeda had planned to destroy in the Millennium Plot,[32] the North Tower mimicked and mocked the holy minaret from which the faithful men are called to prayer five times a day as they submit themselves to Allah's control, which is called His Will. In addition, according to Islamic law, no infidel is permitted to build a home or building that is bigger and better than those of a Muslim. Further, that which is experienced as mocking must be annihilated, not just simply destroyed. Unable to mourn his city's loss of "ancient purity," Atta chose to be embattled on his mother madina's behalf. Indeed, his German master's thesis in urban planning was specifically devoted to the subject of the impact of Westernization (or, as his title put it, urban renewal) on an ancient

Islamic city. He also dedicated his thesis to Allah. He was clearly obsessed by his maternal fusion as it was made manifest in concrete ways.

In Sawyer's documentary, Dr. Ann Graves, a classmate of Atta's in flight school, provides another important clue to his personality. She described him as being without any affect and fixated when he took over the controls in the flight simulator or during real flights. The only time she saw him show any emotion was when she happened to walk in on Atta and Jarrah in the computer room. She found them hugging and jumping up and down with glee like little children. Little did she know that they had just learned of the successful suicide terrorist attack on the USS *Cole*.

At twenty-three years old, Marwan Al-Sheyhi was the youngest terrorist when he flew into the South Tower of the World Trade Center. Some sources report that he was Atta's cousin or nephew. He may have been both because of the Arab custom of marrying within the family (*bint am*, or cousin marriage as the best kind of marriage). There is also the repeated pattern in Al-Qaeda of family members participating together in the same terrorist cell, indicating that they subscribed to the importance of blood relations as a sought-after source of trust. Al-Sheyhi's German teacher, Frau Bach, who first met him when he moved to Bonn at age eighteen, fondly remembered Marwan. She described him in cherubic terms: fun loving, relaxed, and jovial. Two years later he moved to Hamburg to be with Atta and Jarrah and then traveled with them to Afghanistan to undergo training at Osama bin Laden's camps. Upon their return, the three sported the sign of this exclusive Afghan alumni club—the famous beard.[33] While Al-Sheyhi was not a leader, nonetheless, he seemed to work well with Atta.[34]

Has it been too reductive thus far to claim that the Early Mother plays a critical role for these Death Pilots? By looking at the meaning of the group's name in Arabic and what two Arab authorities have to say, the answer may be more evident. While it is easy to trace the name back to Abdallah Azzam's Al-Qaeda al-Sulbah (The Solid Base), this link does not tell us its unconscious significance. Turning to dictionary entries and using one's imagination, it becomes clearer. One of its dictionary entries is "base," as in the geographic place where a military force refuels and gets its supplies. Burke writes, "It can mean a base, as in a camp or a home, or a foundation such as what is under a house. It can mean a pedestal that supports a column. It can also mean a precept, rule principle, maxim, formula, method, model or pattern." He also notes that in slang it can mean database, as in the registry Osama bin Laden created to keep track of the mujahideen who visited his guesthouses as their families often tried to learn of their fate.[35] But the most revealing commentary on the meaning of the meaning of Al-Qaeda and its connection to *ummi*, "the mommy," comes from bin Laden himself: "So this place was called 'The Base,' as in a training base, and the name grew from this. We aren't separated from the ummah. We are the children of the ummah, and an inseparable part of it."[36] Ummah and ummi are practically synonymous, at the very least, in fantasy. They come from the same root, indicating that the mother looms large in the Arab Muslim psyche.

This description of Al-Qaeda's meaning sounds similar to that of the good Early Mother as the foundation of life. It should also be recalled that Hani Hanjour's father was a food supplier, providing the basics of life. Arabic further confirms the association since it must draw on a root system in order to build meaning. The word "Al-Qaeda" is heard up against its semantic field, which serves as a kind of unconscious linguistic backdrop. Jacques Lacan has claimed that the unconscious is structured just as language is[37]; however, one does not have to ascribe to Lacanian psychoanalysis to understand that a person is born into language, is bathed in it early on, and will die in it. Language is the cultural repository of a people. Knowing all the subtleties of a language is very difficult for the nonnative speaker. In Arabic, the root for the word "Al-Qaeda" is *qaf-ayin-dal* (to sit). When spoken or read by the native Arabic speaker, it is a mere hop, skip, and jump from Al-Qaeda to its semantic cousin *Qa'iida*, which means "a woman companion, wife or spouse."[38] Thus, built into the mother tongue of these Death Pilots' mind-set, another maternal cameo surfaces. The base is the mother, wife, and provider for Osama bin Laden and his men, who wish to be completely taken care of as if they were infants.

What happens when Mama doesn't provide? What does a disgruntled and fused group do with its rage? It finds a scapegoat, or the so-called sacred martyr, who purges the group of its mounting rage, which threatens to dissolve the group fusion. The term "scapegoat" originally referred to a goat set loose in the wilderness after a religious leader symbolically laid the sins of the people upon its head. It currently refers to any group or individual who is made to bear the blame for others. Because unresolved rage threatens to dissolve the group fusion, a sacred scapegoat—in this case, a suicide bomber—is chosen to target and direct the group's murderous rage on to the victims. Whether the victims are Jews, Christians, Sunnis, or Shiites, the end is the same—mass murder. The martyr must be held sacred because the fused group and its leader harbor unbearable shame and guilt.

Turning to one of the leading Arab experts on domestic violence and the senior lecturer at the Hebrew University in Jerusalem's School of Social Work, Mohammed Haj-Yahia has documented an epidemic of domestic violence linked to the intifadas, which is where we also find suicidal terrorism.[39] This research dovetails with the Centre for Social Cohesion's findings in the United Kingdom that where jihadis were located, there was overlap with honor killing, or the unique subset of domestic violence for Arab and Asian cultures linked to Islam.[40] Given the fact that honor killings are socially sanctioned murders, the culture has never sought to contain this unconscious rage stemming from early childhood. Murdering young girls and women has concretized blaming the other. In the 2008 study *Crimes of the Community: Honour-based Violence in the United Kingdom*, James Brandon and Salam Hafez noted that law enforcement did geo-mapping for honor killing and where terrorists lived. There was an overlap.[41] While an absolute link may not be established as yet, this information is one more instance of evidence pointing to the link between violence in the home and externalized violence of the jihadis. License to blame the wife or daughter as if she were the Early Mother is a given. Such an unconscious mind-set also encourages mass murder of the other—namely, the Jew or Christian. While honor killing generally involves the murder of the daughter, that the murder occurs within the family underscores the obsessive fixation with the female, be it the daughter or the wife.

Turning to the leading authority concerning Palestinian suicide bombers, Dr. Eyad Sarraj of Gaza has identified the central psychological problem: "I have the feeling that most of these people [the suicide bombers] had a problem with power, either in their childhood or later on. People generally strive for power and want to be in control. This is the ultimate power, controlling life and death."[42]

It may be difficult for some readers to connect the dots between the maternal symbiotic tie and its relationship to pathological control, which leads to a "power" problem. Infants feel so completely helpless and dependent upon their mothers that they compensate for their frustration through becoming grandiose and omnipotent, believing unconsciously that they control everything and everyone. Most infants grow out of this phase fairly early. Some never do.

You might ask, is it fair to equate the Palestinian suicide murderers with the Death Pilots of September 11? When asked this very question, Dr. Sarraj replied: "These [nineteen suicide murderers] could be people who came from a similar kind of environment but who underwent a certain kind of training. [Furthermore] being Muslim and facing the same kind of feelings of being victims in relation to Israeli and American power" led those people to the "maximum exercise of power against the world's only superpower."[43]

Exerting this kind of control is schizoid. R. D. Laing wrote: "Such a person is not able to experience himself 'together with' others or 'at home in' the world."[44] Taking comfort in such hard, inanimate objects as airplanes, computers, cell phones, knives, and box cutters, the terrorists protected themselves, and by adhering to a rigid, black-and-white world of rules similar to those that Atta reiterated in his final letters the night before the mission, they had no room to think autonomously as mature individuals. Tolerating being in a group only temporarily, they led double lives as the enemy among us, stalking us and preying on us just as a disgruntled husband or jilted lover would. They manipulated the system to their own malevolent ends. They had all even obtained Social Security numbers in order to appear to have legitimate identities in America.[45]

The fourth Death Pilot, Ziad Samir Jarrah, offers the best example of the concretized maternal cameo. Moreover, Jarrah was the only pilot who failed in his mission when he crashed in Pennsylvania. A dashing young man of twenty-nine who moved to Germany to study, he had a beautiful and highly accomplished fiancée named Aysel Sengun, a German born of Turkish Muslim parents. He had it all.[46] He came from a modern, wealthy Lebanese Muslim home. He even attended an elite Catholic high school in cosmopolitan, though politically unstable, Beirut. He was the only brother among four sisters. In Sawyer's documentary, Jarrah is seen dancing at one of his sister's weddings surrounded by this gynarchy. His high school science teacher revealingly noted that Jarrah's relationship with girls was something "special."

This description immediately reminded me of a former patient who was a highly successful businessman and the eldest son of a large family with many sisters. My patient explained to me that his sisters felt he completely understood them. He took great pride in this description, believing that he knew what empathy was. Yet his thinking was clearly delusional because he could not accept the fact that his wife of twelve years fled from him one day, leaving a note citing his intolerable, controlling behavior.

Jarrah also became increasingly controlling of his fiancée when he returned to Germany after his Afghan training. He wanted her to be more observant of their religion. Meanwhile, his elderly German landlady insisted on painting his portrait, saying, "Ziad, your beard is so dark, it's so dark. You've become a man."

As I watched her recount her story about Ziad to Forrest Sawyer in the documentary, I recalled another time in German history and shuddered in horror, thinking of Germany's perverse fascination with the dark-eyed, dark-haired Semite, the erotic and exotic Oriental, who within a short period of time around the Dreyfus Affair (1894–1906), suddenly fell from grace and became the evil other, or another version of the Early Mother. This kind of transformation is a further example of splitting: when the idealized other (the good Early Mother) falls from grace, she becomes the evil other (the bad Early Mother). Before the Dreyfus Affair, the Jew was identified as the other, who at first was idealized by German society as exotic and erotic.[47] But when the

Jew fell from grace around the time of the Dreyfus trial, the Jew was equated to the female and viewed as evil.[48] Similarly, the Prophet Muhammad had first courted the Jews, adapting their bible and legends into his message, hoping to be recognized as their messiah. When they rejected him, they fell from grace and became the evil other.

There remains pervasive ambivalence in Germany to this day concerning the foreign other, which today is embodied in the *gastarbeiters* (guest workers), such as the Turks and the Kurds. Indeed, during the 1980s, the Germans wrote about my doctoral work on the sixteenth-century Aljamiado-Morisco literature of the last Muslim enclave in the West precisely because they sensed that the Kurds and the Turks were not integrating into German society. They had instead created their own parallel universe.[49]

The Germans' fascination with the other also revealed their guilt and ambivalence. It was not mere happenstance that Mohammed Atta could build a terrorist cell in Hamburg before relocating to the United States. Playing on German guilt about the Holocaust, the Death Pilots could play the victim card as foreigners, hide behind lenient German privacy laws, and make their plans of mass destruction.[50]

But Jarrah, meanwhile, was also in conflict. It was on his flight that the passengers used their cell phones to call loved ones. Were they told to do so one last time? If so, was it because of how he had led on his fiancée, letting her think they still had a future? Jarrah had made plans with her and had called his father five times the day he had sent her to Lebanon, seeking approval for their marriage.[51]

Jarrah also called his surrogate mother, his landlady, two days before the attack. He even called his fiancée the morning of the attack, promising her that he would call back that afternoon. He also sent her a farewell letter. All of these anxious attempts to connect one last time in fantasy with his mother also underscore the attacking sadism of the suicide's sadism, which is inflicted on those left behind. In other words, these Death Pilots were very angry with their mothers for not nurturing them the way they wanted. Suicide is both masochistic because it destroys the self and sadistic because it attacks those who are left behind, such as their mothers, who now have to deal with the guilt over their sons' deaths.

Phone calls aside, an Arabic poem Hezbollah made popular when Jarrah was a boy in Beirut tells of a mother who busies herself with her son's wedding plans. The son abruptly tells her that he will not marry; instead, the appointed day will mark his death: "The day I meet the black-eyed virgins [will be] my wedding, in this world [it] is my day of martyrdom; and the blood on my face is my decoration."[52] Lacking the capacity for metaphor as well as the ability to contain his rage, Jarrah and the others literally acted out the poem in their martyrs' marriage of suicide and homicide.

One wonders, too, if culturally embedded in the figure of the Islamic suicide bomber is the Arabic *jinn* (known to the West as the genie made famous by Aladdin's lamp). The comparison holds because the jinn is a spirit that often appears in human form and carries out the wishes of its summoner, and that is exactly what Jarrah and the other Death Pilots of September 11 did for Al-Qaeda. Yet unfortunately, unlike Aladdin's genies, once uncapped, the figure of the Islamic suicide bomber can never be expunged from human memory. Only when the umma, the worldwide Islamic community in all its diversity, assumes responsibility and acknowledges its role in promoting and advancing this kind of political domestic violence in the human family can the rage of Islamic suicidal terrorism be contained.

4

OSAMA BIN LADEN

Political Violence and
Islamic Suicidal Terrorism

A man and a woman together are like a live ember by the side of
a mine of gun powder.
— *The Light* (Muslim periodical)

Metaphorically speaking, when a man and a woman are together, they become a mixture of love and hate. The hate and resulting sadism may become a more pervasive factor than love; the involvement escalates to violence. Acts of Islamic suicidal terrorism are a political mixture of hatred and unconscious love because political domestic violence is paranoid group behavior. When this mixture of feelings happens, it follows that two different groups—the terrorists and their targeted victims—may symbolically "wed," just as a couple weds. As such, suicide and murder may occur, expressing the mutual groups' fantasy of domestic violence.[1] Because suicide terrorism is so pervasive today, even the unknowing innocent may harbor fantasies of suicide terrorism. The terrorists from the Arab Muslim world feel that they need to see America as the evil partner responsible for all the world's problems.[2] They envision her as the exciting seductive, enviable, threatening, and dangerous object of their envy, fear, and hatred, which intrudes upon and disrupts Arab unity. It is their fantasy of her, their terror about being dependent upon her, and their feeling of incompetence that disrupt Arab unity as a false harmony.

The violence, as noted in previous chapters, is related to the high levels of child and spouse abuse in Islamic societies. Since domestic violence reenacts "the seething cauldron of erotic, passionate, and murderous emotions within the family," it lends itself well to a psychoanalytic inquiry about conjoint murder-suicide.[3]

The world has witnessed one of the most abusive "couple" relationships ever, that of the unconscious, pathological "love affair" between Osama bin Laden and the United States. From the beginning, Bin Laden and his entourage of Islamic suicide bombers have engaged in the perverted dance of political domestic violence. By "wedding" themselves to Christians and Jews through suicide and murder, they have reversed the usual order of domestic violence, where the object of hatred and love is murdered first prior to the suicide. By proxy, as bin Laden sends out terrorists on their missions, he vicariously participates in suicidal terrorism from a distance. We do not see him or any of his "offspring" participating in the Death Pilot's role. This is the nature of perverse love: bin Laden fans the flames of rage while the suicide bombers seek a unique, symbolic maternal fusion in death.

Delusionally envious of America, bin Laden felt betrayed by the United States when Saudi Arabia called on it to rescue Saudi Arabia and Kuwait from Iraq in 1990–1991. From his perspective, he was both entitled and obligated to be the savior of his Saudi Arabian homeland, leading the mujahideen forces that had fought with him in Afghanistan. Bin Laden responded to this rejection with lethal fear and rage. However, Amrika, the Arabic female name that Osama bin Laden uses, has a life of her own and chooses not to be submissive to his will. Bin Laden and his entourage feel mocked by America; therefore, as much as they lust after Amrika, they must destroy her.

Bin Laden has submitted his "holy" self to Allah, yet his other self maintains a lustful, unconscious attachment to America and the values she represents. America may remind him of his first girlfriend, Rita, a Christian he met in cosmopolitan Beirut during his days of binge drinking.[4] Bin Laden's relationship with Amrika is not a far cry from that of couples traumatically bonded in marital conflict.

We see throughout this study a major recurring theme of shame, humiliation, and disgrace. Not only did bin Laden feel snubbed by King Fahd bin Abdul Aziz and humiliated by America's soldiers bivouacked on holy Saudi soil,[5] but in bin Laden's videotape of October 7, 2001, he made a dramatic reference to Islam itself being humiliated and disgraced. Avner Falk has linked this explicit historical reference to the fall of the Ottoman sultanate in 1918 as the last great vestige of the Muslim empires: "In his mind, bin Laden *was* Islam. He too had suffered 'humiliation and disgrace' throughout his early life."[6] Hence, bin Laden's cri de coeur is, "Islam and I are one."

Psychoanalysis recognizes that often a person is unable to make a clear distinction between the self and the other, thus constituting a merger or fusion. Bin Laden is merged with his conception of the Arab people, which dovetails with the Arab ideology of *asabiya* (group solidarity and loyalty that informs the Arab sense of honor.) Such a merger superficially bolsters his weak internal sense of self, which already feels humiliated.

Malise Ruthven notes that the main ideologue for bin Laden and Al-Qaeda was the Egyptian Islamist theologian, Said Qutb, who also was polarized by his experience in the West. Unwittingly, Qutb revealed how sexually threatened he had felt there and even accused the Central Intelligence Agency (CIA) and the Federal Bureau of Investigation (FBI) of trying to seduce him with a "drunken, semi-naked" female agent:

> The importance he accorded the incident, however, is itself significant: he must have felt some attraction for the woman since, as his biographer put it, "the encounter successfully tested his resolve to resist experiences damaging to his identity as an Egyptian and a Muslim." For a virgin (one presumes) of 42, this direct encounter with female sexuality "in the raw" was profoundly unsettling.[7]

Qutb penned *Signposts on the Road* while he was imprisoned for an assassination attempt on Gamal Abdel Nasser's life in 1954. His writings reveal his murderous rage. It would go on to be concretized in the Islamist's act of supposed martyrdom—that is, killing in the name of God—which is an act of theological sadomasochism.

This sadomasochism is also very similar to the violence couples experience when they are enmeshed in conflicts that end with the estranged lovers murdering their girlfriends and then committing suicide. It expresses the desperate and unspoken mutual terrors of abandonment, engulfment, and merging as well as the mutual desire to be taken care of like an infant even though it also involves excruciating shame and humiliation.[8]

Murderous rage defends against unconscious infantile love. The little boy who builds a tower out of toy blocks and strikes it down in one fell swoop while yelling, "I hate you!" at his mother is really saying the opposite: "I love you, Mommy, and I'm scared." What is he terrified about? Overwhelming feelings of dependency and neediness, terror of abandonment, vulnerability, shame, humiliation, and helplessness—all of it is terrorizing for the little boy. This same little boy grows up, falls in love, and marries. At some point he begins to hate his wife. The love affair has gone sour. Keeping this imaginary vignette in mind, we can continue to explore the psychodynamics of Islamic suicidal terrorism as an expression of the adult's terrors, which are similar to that of the little boy's. But when acted out, the destructiveness of their rage is made concrete because of an impaired sense of reality. The terrorists have mistaken their murderous thoughts for reality.

Osama bin Laden, the nineteen hijackers of September 11, Al-Qaeda, the PLO's Yasir Arafat, and the members of Hamas, Islamic Jihad, the Al-Aqsa Martyrs' Brigade, and Hezbollah, along with their limitless supply of suicide bombers, have actually "fallen in love" with America and Israel, but they cannot admit it. Instead, they act as two-year-olds do because they cannot recognize, articulate, or accept their feelings. They are also confused about their gender identity. Among the men, it is a common problem, especially for men who abuse their partners in domestic violence. They are especially fearful that they are homosexual or, even worse, that by the actual, real touch of a woman in the wrong place at the wrong time, they will lose their masculinity. Their rage and need to blame are very similar to that of the little boy and his blocks, though the hope is that the little boy will grow up, be able to contain his rage in an appropriate way, and be aware of his destructive fantasies. As a mature adult, he will perhaps think of them but not act them out as a jilted lover or a delusionally jealous husband would. For most people, murderous rage is fantasized and even thought about, consciously or unconsciously, but it is not acted out in real time by annihilating innocent civilians.

The political violence of Islamic suicide terrorism is related to the high levels of child and wife abuse and battery, including honor killings in conjunction with the practice of misogyny in Islamic societies.[9] None of this family violence has been seriously addressed in terrorism studies. Not unrelated to the contagious effect that such violence is known to have, there has been a kind of mirror-image phenomenon with increased domestic violence among the American military personnel returning home from special operations in Iraq and Afghanistan, as well as a recent surge of family violence in Israel that has been linked to the political violence of the suicide bombings and soaring economic hardship the country has faced. In the sports culture of the United States, it is an empirically documented phenomenon that domestic violence also increases on Super Bowl football weekends.[10] The Centers for Disease Control state that one quarter of American women experience domestic violence.[11] No community or socioeconomic class is immune from this phenomenon, which stems from problems in early maternal attachment yet is played out in heterosexual or homosexual relationships later on in life. That familiarity and exposure are precisely why all of us relate and react to the Islamic suicide attack—because we share this commonality and strategic threat. Unchecked aggression spreads like wildfire, like a contagion.

The violent hatred shown by bin Laden, Death Pilot Muhammad Atta, and Qutb is related to two important matters concerning identity development. First, it involves the defining of one's self against the other. Second, the violence expresses an unconscious and, for lack of a better word, primitive love or attraction—that is, a libidinal desire—for the other.[12] It has been noted that Arabic comes from the root *ayin-ra-ba*, as in the name *Arab*, which means "eloquence." The "other" is called *Ajam*, meaning "unintelligibility." It is similar to the Greek notion of the other being the babbling barbarian. For Islamists, this "us versus them" mentality holds a more extreme view of the other as a pagan (*jahiliya*), with the added inflection of the lewd or sexually provocative. Thus, the bad influence of American culture, which the Islamists vociferously deride, masks their excitement of how unconsciously enthralled, tempted, and confused they are by such freedom that America represents.

The conscious, deliberate decision to deploy the weapon of the suicide bomber is not mutually exclusive with the unconscious of the group and the individual selves of the terrorists. In fact, they are coextensive, and together this combination is lethally synergistic.

Be it Robert Pape's *Dying to Win: The Strategic Logic of Suicide Terrorism* or Scott Atran's "The Genesis of Suicide Terrorism," only a small part of the complex phenomena is examined by these proposed theories, which overlook the force of fantasy and culture.[13] Pape is correct when he asserts that terrorism is about liberation, but it is not just seeking liberation for one's motherland. It is also quite literally and concretely battling for liberation from the Early Mother. Such liberation can also be reality based.

Palestinian psychiatrist Shalfic Masalqa, who has studied suicide bombers, makes the important point that if an adult is secure in his or her sense of identity, he or she cannot be humiliated.[14] While Masalqa does take the notion of shame and humiliation of early childhood into account, there is virtually no discussion of this aspect with regard to the early maternal experience in the Arab Muslim world. We know that the first three years of life are crucial for the development of a happy, healthy child, yet there has been almost no discussion concerning the impact of physical, sexual, and emotional abuse and battery or the quality of maternal attachment and traumatic bonding on the child's development. Nor has there been any discussion about how these factors in child-rearing practices have given rise to Islamic suicide terrorism in light of other distinct cultural practices and beliefs about the family and most especially about the Early Mother of these terrorists within Islam.

Normative Islam does not promote Islamic suicide terrorism, but its parenting and cultural practices can and do. This connection is part of the reason why drawing such a tight distinction between that which is Arab and that which is Muslim is a specious argument. They are inextricably bound together. Furthermore, the umma outside of Saudi Arabia considers and venerates as the "true" Islam all that is deemed "Arab" in Saudi culture.

The frequency of suicide terrorism being linked to a majority of Muslim terrorist organizations is high, as mentioned earlier. The reluctance of counterterrorism experts to engage in a serious discussion of the implication of early childhood development and maternal attachment is another telling sign of resistance and discomfort because such a discussion takes them out of their comfort zone. Yet patterns of group fantasies are known to be crucial for a sense of identity. Shame and humiliation are key emotional experiences for the individual and the group that have been at the center of psychohistory's discussion concerning the repetition of childhood traumatic experience under the guise of political violence. It has been noted how terrorists attach to their charismatic leader and participate in a paranoid delusion, thus alleviating their persecutory anxieties through political violence.[15]

The foundational narratives of the Bible and the Quran, respectively, have been investigated as being cornerstones of the shame, humiliation, and guilt fueling the Arab-Israeli conflict, with two sides being viewed as a dysfunctional couple.[16] Other work has demonstrated how Muslim Turkish children learn early in their lives how to externalize their bad feelings of shame and humiliation and project them on to the other. It has also been shown how there can be an uncanny fit between approved cultural practices and group fantasies that serve to reinforce the tendency to externalize, project, and blame others rather than learning to contain one's negative, painful, and shameful feelings.[17] Falk has traced out in detail the persecutory anxieties, shame, and humiliation arising out of the maternal relationship that cause a weakened sense of self, which then cannot separate psychologically from the mother. Hence, group identity later becomes hyper-valued as ethno-nationalism or religious orthodoxy. These bonds are attempts to compensate for an insecure maternal attachment by means of substitute identities. They too externalize and split the world into an infantile love-hate relationship as seen in the case of Islamic terrorist groups. It is a conflict-habituated relationship.[18]

How might suicide bombers alleviate their unbearable desires and urges? I suggest that it may be by means of the unconscious defense mechanism of dual projective identification:[19] the split-off bad and unwanted parts of the self are projected on to the hated, evil other in a reciprocal way, recycling an unending hatred and violence with moments of perverse pleasure in the sado-masochistic glue of traumatic bonding. What one hates most about one's self is split off, projected on to the other, and uncannily not recognized. Then the other is attacked over it. The murderous rage against the other is thus really against the other of the self, which has been disavowed, or one's persecutory internal objects. The dynamic harks back to a specific dimension of the first relationship in life with the mother—namely, the early maternal fusion. Melanie Klein described the paranoid-schizoid experiences of the infant vacillating between eros and violence as well as between merger and separation.[20] Today we speak in terms of maternal attachment problems—especially those that are disorganized and chaotic—about a kind of traumatic bonding.

In the family of nations, there has been a similar behavior pattern, ranging from blaming America and Israel to boycotting them to offering support and empathy. America and Israel have also been accused of causing the shame and humiliation that the Islamists feel. Why is there this widespread difference in responses? How can we understand the blaming?

The answer may be found in people's unconscious identifications—some with the aggressor and some with the victim, as we all ambivalently identify with both at times—which lead to their immobilizing confusion and unconscious guilt. This conflict causes a kind of paralysis that inhibits a person's ability to state firmly that suicide terrorism is wrong and counter to the norms of acceptable human behavior. Murder is murder.

Instead, then, the debate deteriorates into blaming the murder victim. The murder is defensively justified by such a response as "Well, they [Israel and America] do it too." As superpowers that engage military force to set limits on unacceptable behavior, Israeli and U.S. forces' operations do result in a regrettable loss of civilian life. Yet blaming the victim of suicide terrorist acts remains an uncanny tactic both to shift the focus away from the aberrant ter-rorist behavior and to attempt to justify the behavior of those terrorist groups that engage in methods and actions associated with the Mafia, religious cults, and prostitution rings—all of which are criminal groups.

Shame and humiliation are the responses to painful feelings when the failure of a sexualized fantasy or object fails to provide protection.[21] The shame-blame game in the political arena of terrorism is a misplaced projection of deep-seated sexualized fantasies embraced by the blaming culture. These erotized fantasies function as obstacles to achieving a better standard of liv-ing because of conflict. They do not allow for assuming mature responsibility for finding creative ways to promote change, which its members are able and competent enough to do. The erotic dimension lurking behind the scene of any kind of political violence is rarely discussed, even though experts know there is a sadomasochistic dimension to violence that intersects with gender and sexuality. To give just one example, it was related to me that the Taliban often work in groups of twelve men with a "thirteenth man"—who is just a boy—designated for rape.[22] Yet in discussions with regard to the jihadis' pro-files, no one acknowledges this conduct.

In Islam, a mother's first-born son is her most important child. His birth automatically enhances her status within the community. The firstborn son receives the most of everything: love, attention, material goods, and so on. The only person in the family who has more status than the firstborn son is his father. (In the case of honor killings, a girl's oldest brother has the most power because he is tasked with carrying out the honor murder.) The firstborn son is the mother's only source of power albeit by vicarious proxy. Indeed, it is common for a little sister in an Arab Muslim family to believe, at first, that her eldest brother is married to their mother and that he is her father![23] The im-portance of the family in understanding jihadi violence cannot be overstated. Halim Barakat has written, "Arab society, then, is the family generalized or enlarged, and the family is society in miniature."[24]

The figure of the mother looms larger than life for both the Arab and the Muslim family because the word "ummi" (mommy) shares the same Arabic root as umma, or the Arabic name for the Muslim community. The shared root unconsciously magnifies the enormity and significance of the maternal. The umma sanctions and supports the jihadis' kind of political violence throughout Europe, Africa, Asia, and the Americas because it remains by and large silent on condemning their mass murders. This silence is the essence of passive-aggressive behavior. That is, the umma's refusal to intervene on the victim's behalf allows the passive-aggressive umma to relish inflicting pain on the victim in this peculiar manner while at the same time slyly denying that it has done anything wrong. How dare anyone accuse the umma of such behavior? Even though there is great diversity within the umma, its members tend to justify murderous behavior without any genuine reflection concerning it.

But why does this willingness to collude with the perpetrator happen? Judith Herman explains it in the following manner: "It is very tempting to take the side of the perpetrator. All the perpetrator asks is that the bystander [the umma—addition mine] do nothing. He appeals to the universal desire to see, hear, and speak no evil. The victim, on the contrary, asks the bystander to share the burden of pain. The victim demands action, engagement, and re-membering."[25]

Because Hamida, Osama bin Laden's mother, was so devalued, the only way she could feel strong with regard to her husband Muhammad bin Awad bin Laden and his huge harem and family was to identify her power, aggression, and rage through her son. She was victimized by her husband. The harem, the mother-son bond, and scapegoating need to be understood in a primitive and biological, or ancestral, sense. (Curiously, the only other primate that has a harem is the gorilla.[26]) Bin Laden exemplifies the results of these psycho-dynamics and identifications. He projects his rage outward against the "bad mother," Amrika, as he fights against his derisive nickname, *Ibn al abeda* (Son of the Slave), which his fifty-three or fifty-four siblings gave him. His father's other wives called his mother *al abeda* (the Slave) because she complained about her status as the fourth wife—the one who can be legally discarded but is still financially supported and controlled—as her husband's attention turned elsewhere shortly after Osama's birth.

The wedding of son to mother, as in the case of bin Laden and his mother, sets the stage for the "wedding" of groups. Since groups are known to have "group selves," it follows that two different groups may be seen as symbolically wedded, as if they were a couple. Such a wedding by violence stems from paranoia and is fueled by dual projective identifications.[27] The rhetoric surfacing in discussions of terrorism with regard to the Arab-Israeli conflict, for example, often deploys the idea of the Palestinians and Israelis not being able to separate; hence, the *gader ha-frada*, "fence of separation," was built to set a boundary between the divorcing peoples.[28] It is no different with Al-Qaeda when it expresses its hatred for America and Israel and blames them for all the world's problems. In *A Fury for God: The Islamist Attack on America*, Ruthven concludes that there is not so much a clash between the West and Islam; rather, the so-called clash resides within the Islamist who externalizes his identity crisis and emotional turmoil along with his murderous rage as he projects it outward and enacts it by murdering innocent civilians.

Both domestic violence and political domestic violence involve this wedding of violence between partners. Through the process of the unconscious defense mechanism of dual projective identification described earlier, the self and the other bond in an unending cycle of hatred and violence. Instead of a healthy dependency forming in the first relationship, this fusion transforms not only into a reciprocal hatred between mother and son but, additionally, to a mutual, sadistic attacking. This situation gives rise to a perfect fit for a masochistic, victimized mother who can identify her aggression only through her grandiose, sadistic son.[29]

An example of this behavior can be found in bin Laden's projection of his rage outward against Amrika as he tries to rise above his derisive nickname, Ibn al abeda. Could this "slave" slur be a reference to Hamida, the Berber slave and mother of Musa al-Kazim (The Forbearing), who was the Seventh Imam of the Twelver Shi'a Islam?[30] Could the slur have precipitated an early, unspoken identification for Osama bin Laden with the martyr syndrome of Shia Islam, which gave Islamic suicide terrorism to the world?

Having heard his mother's bitter complaints, bin Laden was aware of his mother's lowly status as the fourth wife. (His billionaire father's estimated fifty-three or fifty-four children were the product of more than the four wives allowed to a Muslim man.) Hence, bin Laden has since been his mother's champion, fighting her battles as he splits off his hatred of the bad Early Mother and projects it on to Amrika.[31]

Islamic suicidal terrorism perceives America and Israel as nation-states having group selves identified with Christianity and Judaism, even though they, too, are part of the extended monotheistic family descended from the same biblical father, Abraham. In 1998, bin Laden formed an alliance with Ayman al-Zawahiri and declared a fatwa of global jihad against the Jews and the Crusaders, showing his group's need to have enemies and perhaps some religious "sibling rivalry."

The group's fatwa is important for several reasons. Its language reveals a grandiose group self stuck in a narcissistic, medieval time warp but using modern technology and organization. The word "Crusader" is an explicit reference to the Muslim Moors' military defeat in Al-Andalus in southern Spain, which was Islam's westernmost caliphate, and their military withdrawal to North Africa. The Muslim Moors' loss of Al-Andalus caused a severe narcissistic injury.[32] Their retreat to North Africa's Maghreb was doubly painful because Islam's establishment of Al-Andalus had been the result of the Muslim Moors' military invasion and subsequent conquest of the indigenous Christian Spanish population in 711 C.E. They had waged jihad to spread Islam and at times had resorted to forced conversion of the conquered peoples. They had conducted a Muslim crusade and stayed for seven hundred years.

The sole objective of the modern Salafi and Wahhabi jihadis is to reinstitute the caliphate at the global level. Ever since the defeat of the Ottoman Empire in 1924 and Kemal Ataturk's secularization of Turkey, the radical Islamists have been smarting and licking their wounds. Losing the "crown jewel" exposed the group to its own impotence. Bin Laden and Zawahiri, the so-called brains behind the jihadis, both talked about reconquering Al-Andalus, demonstrating their group inability to mourn loss.[33] They expressed a desire for a new conquest of Europe.[34] Just as the charismatic leader who refracts political reality through the traumatic lens of his early childhood experience, bin Laden has revealed his maternal fusion without knowing it. Falk predicted something close to this inability to mourn the loss of Al-Andalus,[35] which Akbar Ahmed named "the Andalus Syndrome."[36]

In seeking to reconquer Europe and reestablish the caliphate, marriage, martyrdom, and blood are intimately linked together for the terrorist group. Like the two sides of a coin, the terrorist group has a true self and a false self. The true group self is oriented toward the umma, or private Islamic community. It calls the suicide bomber a shahid, his act the Ars al-Shahada, and his nuptial smile, or *bassamat al-Farah*. Indeed, Mohammed Atta explicitly wrote about the wedding in the detailed instructions he gave to his fellow Death Pilots so they could prepare themselves for the 9/11 attacks: "8. Let your breast be filled with gladness, for there is nothing between you and your wedding but mere seconds."[37]

Instead of grieving, the celebration of the martyr's marriage by the family and clan guarantees more aggression and violence. Mourning is necessary to process the rage of loss. In Lebanese Shiite communities, there are even female martyrs who are named the Brides of Blood (*arous dam*). By using such pseudonyms, the false group self defends against its most violent fantasies, covering up its underlying profound shame and humiliation anxieties.[38] By proxy, the group leader acts vicariously through the suicide bomber. The leader must monitor and purge the group's mounting aggression and rage before it implodes.[39] The false group self provokes the family of humankind but specifically targets the Crusader and Jewish cousin-brides.

Since suicide is self-murder, murder and suicide occurring together are best conceptualized as an extended self-murder, fusing the victim to the murderer. Death concretizes the fusion. While murder was once perceived as the perpetrator acting out a desire to kill the sadistic Oedipal father, Falk has shown that this assumption is not so.[40] Rather, the assassin wishes to kill the sadistic Early (pre-Oedipal) Mother. The murder's emotional turmoil is that of the terrified infant at the whim of its mother. The inability to mourn the loss of the maternal fusion leaves the adult terrorized at the deepest level, having internalized the Early Mother as a terrorist. The suicide bomber displays a graphic road map of these psychodynamics.

What is it about the maternal symbiosis that stirs up such violence? The Early Mother is experienced as voluptuous: the baby feels excited and alive and experiences the warmth of eros. As described in chapter 1, the baby is nurtured by the good breast, which becomes associated with the good Early Mother. When the baby feels abruptly abandoned, he or she experiences sheer terror, which leads to the baby splitting his or her perceptions of the mother. This splitting is the basis for paranoia.[41] Fearful and anxiously attached, the infant clings to the traumatic maternal bond, or fusion, for something is better than nothing. Domestic violence is the couple's expression of this infantile terror, as the partners mutually project and recycle endlessly the terror tinged with eros. Feeling out of control, fearing the pull of regression to the early voluptuous mother, homicide-suicide erupts.[42]

It is my contention that Osama bin Laden and his suicide bombers display similar terrors. Even William Shakespeare captured the Islamic propensity toward traumatic bonding in *Othello*, a drama featuring a sixteenth-century military Moor who suffers from delusional jealousy.

The main ingredient for this delusion is predicated on a young son having no rival. In Islamic culture, the mother raises a young boy away from his father until age seven; he is kept solely in the company of women. The son believes irrationally that he owns his mother, as he would a piece of property, and that he rules the world, just as bin Laden thinks he does.[43] In his *Sexuality in Islam*, Abdelwahab Bouhdiba argues that there exists a Muslim counterpart to the Western Oedipus complex, the Judar complex, which takes its name from a young man in *One Thousand and One Arabian Nights*. In order to gain his freedom, Judar's mother must disappear, that is, be destroyed. Hence, the tale expresses the violence against the Early Mother, the first female in a man's life. Delusional jealousy, the key precursor of homicide in domestic violence, is intertwined with, but is more annihilating than, envy in conjugal paranoia. For instance, fueling Othello's jealous flames is Iago, who persuades Othello that his wife, Desdemona, has been unfaithful. Othello murders her and kills himself, leading to suicidal domestic violence as sometimes being referred to as the Othello syndrome.

A difficulty with applying the paradigm of domestic violence to bin Laden and the suicide bombers stems from a paucity of information about their childhoods. However, our general knowledge of Islamic childhood and family relations is increasing, as Muslim psychologists courageously step forward to document Islamic domestic violence. They are providing more information on how honor crimes, polygamy, and even the sexual honor of female chastity are used as methods to subjugate women. Isolated from her family in an arranged marriage at a young age, the young Muslim woman fits the profile of the woman at risk, especially under radical Islam and the terrorists.[44]

Bin Laden and his male entourage control their many wives in a preoccupied, obsessive manner, sequestering them at home, targeting them for beatings, and stalking them. Rather than negotiate with a wife, the Islamic fundamentalist simply takes another. The Taliban publicly displayed their terror of the exciting female body by forcing women to revert to the ancient custom of going about fully veiled, covered from head to toe. Afghan women under the Taliban's control cannot expose any flesh reminiscent of the voluptuous, warm Early Mother.

In the Islamic world, women are not the only subjugated group. Non-Muslims—not only Christians and Jews but also Hindus, Buddhists, and others—are never considered equals. Instead, they are always regarded as second-class citizens under a protectorate status known as *dhimmeh* (which will be discussed further in chapter 5). Indeed, *dhimmi* comes from an Arabic root *dhal-mim-mim*, which means "to blame."[45] The only submission that the Muslim participates in for the group, however, is surrendering to Allah, which is what the word "Islam" means. Bin Laden and the suicide bombers merely take this dynamic to the next level. They stalk their victims and conceal their crude weapons for surprise attacks not only at the World Trade Center but also in countless demolished marketplaces, checkpoints, funerals, weddings, police stations, embassies, and pilgrimage rest stops in the Middle East and even against ships at sea.

Yet, the time sequence, the mode of death, and the anonymous victim are unique. As I have noted earlier, in political domestic violence, suicide occurs before the murder. By contrast, in domestic violence, the loved one is killed prior to the murderer committing suicide or setting up a scenario in which he will be killed by the police, not unlike the Filipino *moro*, who is taught to fight to the death. The terrorist kills by controlling the appointed time of the wedding of death; the terrorist kills himself and, by extension, the other. In detonating the charge, be it on a belt or a vehicle turned into a bomb, the suicide bomber embeds himself into his victims, mixing his blood and body parts with theirs. Reminiscent of the moments right before birth—it is as if he were restaging it—the terrorist weds himself to the victim, a stand-in for the exciting, voluptuous, and terrifying Early Mother. In the terrorist's mind's eye, blood is more valuable than breast milk as he forestalls birth through a death fusion. In chapters 6 and 7, we will learn the significance and psychological meaning of the bloody body parts.

When confronted in an interview with the fact that the Prophet Muhammad forbade the killing of innocent women and children, Osama bin Laden replied that the injunction was not absolute and that the Death Pilots achieved a "balance of terror." Thus, by his reasoning, if the West kills the innocent, Al-Qaeda is justified to respond in kind until the West stops. Author Mohammed Hafez has pointed out that this displacement of blame for violence is intended to shift the focus away from one's crimes as well as make the victimizer appear to be the victim.[46] It is a classic example of what the abuser always does—blame the victim. One of the most bewildering things concerning Islamic suicide terrorism is that much of the world does not condemn the use of the suicide bomber. Indeed, much of the world wants instead to appease the terrorists. Many are willing to view the violence as justifiable and acceptable. How can this stance be understood psychologically? Hafez argues that the ideology, which is reframed by the terrorists, causes a moral disengagement that leads to anti-civilian violence. This moral inversion elevates the Al-Qaeda militant to the status of a legitimate defender of rights while it simultaneously deprives his Western victims of innocence and imbues them with culpability.

Moreover, by framing violence as an inevitable manifestation of cruelties and oppression inflicted by the West, Al-Qaeda terrorists are able to relinquish free will and parry the condemnations of their critics.

While Hafez describes well the dynamic of the "you do it too" syndrome—also recognized in the Latin phrase "tu quoque"—he neither links it to domestic violence, where victim blaming occurs all the time, nor names it as paranoia. Furthermore, his word choices are revealing. By calling the Al-Qaeda terrorists militants in one breathe and then terrorists in the next, he himself blurs the distinction between abuser and victim. Doing so, he sabotages his own discourse. Either one is a terrorist or one is a militant, but one cannot be both at the same time.

The Islamic terrorists claim that America, Israel, and their Western allies have superior military capabilities with which the Muslim world cannot compete. They declare that the West has murdered Muslims; therefore, they reason and argue that using the suicide bomber is justifiable. From where does this argument stem psychologically? And what does it attempt to cover up? It speaks to the sense of persecution that haunts those who engage in this kind of behavior. It is also frequently heard in a couple's arguments when the abuser tries to gain the upper hand of the argument by claiming, "But you do it too!" It is merely a diversionary strategy to prevent others from looking more closely at what is happening in the abusive dynamic with its genuine infliction of pain and sadism. Why do they not want to think? Abusers do not want to think because they exhibit predatory behavior.

"He hit me and cried; he raced me to complain" is an Arabic saying that provides a means of exploring this dilemma of moral equivalence. The saying is striking because it demonstrates an awareness that such deceitful behavior does exist and is a known behavior in the Arab Muslim world. On the face of it, the jihadi terrorist-perpetrators claim they are victims. They thus subvert the social norms. The dead and the maimed drop out of the brutal and cruel picture of the attack site. It is a reverse superego—the good guys are bad and the bad guys are perceived as good. The real victim is outrun, and perverse empathy for the alleged downtrodden is obtained via identification with the aggressor. To recognize this symbolic level, to know and understand how it works in the psychology of terrorism, and to be able to educate the public about the ramifications of early childhood development and child-rearing practices are the first steps in uprooting and disarming the terrorists' tactical use of such bomb blasts.[47]

There are three parties involved here: the hitter, the victim, and the audience. The instigator engages in concrete behavior, or hitting, and launches a surprise attack. Then the attacker runs to a third anonymous party and claims that he is the real victim. The real victim voices the Arabic saying after the attack, retrospectively and in the first person. The Arabic saying both describes *and* acknowledges the routine cultural practice of engaging in such distorted behavior. Lopsided regarding the nature of the attack, it notes that the audience that hears the provocateur's complaint has not witnessed the attack. Reminiscent of the bullying brother who runs to his mother to argue his innocence and to accuse his sibling of the brutality, the terrorist tries to get his story out first. His hitting and complaining show that the terrorist feels and believes that the power is made to reside in the other person—the victim—and that the terrorist attacks out of his own fear and envy. The terrorist also tries to negotiate a relationship with the public because he wants the public to fight his battle. His strategy is to shift the blame.

The terrorist is not able to separate out his sense of self from the other on account of his experience with the Early Mother. His sense of self continues to reside in her. His is an adhesive identity as he is glued to her. In adulthood the sense of self continues to reside in the other, whom he attacks. The terrorist persists in being pathologically dependent on the other, who is his targeted enemy. As odd as it might seem, for the terrorist, going on the attack is enlivening. Otherwise, he feels dead, depleted, and deprived and fears that he will fall into a black hole or become a nobody. The terrorist needs to be enraged, to hate, and to have an enemy in order to stabilize this inchoate sense of being. He has a fragile sense of self. The radical ideologies act as a kind of girdle for such a fragile self.

The political violence of suicide terrorism is not sheltered from the dynamic of being male or female. While it is not within the scope of this book to address the female suicide bomber, it is important to point out that it is precisely the issue of gender and sexuality that draws such attention to the female suicide bomber. Yet the issue of sexuality and gender is not explored with regard to the male suicide bomber. It seems that the female suicide bomber literally embodies the hidden desire to talk about the taboo subjects of eros, sadomasochism, and murder in this context. In fact, it is my belief that the attraction of the female suicide bomber is the closest that the public, journalists, and others will allow themselves to approach, by proxy, a genuine discussion of the Early Mother, which the female suicide bomber represents. These women of childbearing age carry bombs instead of babies. Indeed, terrorists make fake casts of pregnant abdomens to disguise the bombs. It is an example of concrete behavior and rage against the prenatal mother, who also represents the fusion of mother and fetus,[48] but there have also been pregnant female suicide bombers. These female bombers have internalized the males' rage of the female as self-rage. The male terrorists are also obsessed with the prenatal mother. A woman is so devalued in their minds that they have trouble understanding how they, macho men, could be born from such a devalued body. We know that the leading cause of death for the prenatal mother in the West is murder by a spouse or partner, accounting for one-third of deaths.[49] To the best of my knowledge no such statistics for the Arab Muslim world are kept concerning the prenatal mother, but the point here is that we can see the commonality of the threat that the prenatal mother poses to those men who essentially feel hopelessly humiliated and esmasculated.

Domestic violence offers a valuable paradigm for organizing the dynamics of love and hate that are involved in the conjoint murder-suicide of Islamic suicidal terrorism by reading the behavior functionally rather than substantially. Be it Palestinian suicide bombers who wear suicide belts or the hijackers of September 11, 2001, who turned airplanes into missiles of mass destruction, they share a striking commonality with the perpetrators of domestic violence. While still speculative because of a lack of adequate information, initial unpublished and noncirculating evidence suggests that in the case of Palestinian female suicide bombers, pathological control is also a significant issue for these women.[50] More likely than not, by appearing as if these women are proactive and in control by seeking death, they were repeating the traumatic abuse experienced in their families and attempting to reverse their sense of being trapped and vulnerable.

Domestic violence expresses the most basic human emotions, which are acted out in extremis by conjoint murder and suicide. Acts of Islamic suicidal terrorism are a political mixture of hatred and unconscious love that acts out paranoid group behavior.

5

BIN LADEN'S CONCUBINES

The Jews and the Crusaders?

*[Unlawful] to you are married women, except such as your right hand
possess [i.e., taken in war, or purchased slaves].*
—*Sura 4:28*

*Fight those who have been given Scripture [the Jews and the Christians] as be-
lieve not in Allah nor the Last Day. . . Follow not the religion of truth [Judaism
or Christianity] until they pay the tribute readily, being brought low.*
—*Sura 9:29*

The Prophet Muhammad endorsed the ancient institution of concubinage after he took Rayhana the Jewess as his concubine following the Battle
of the Trench in A.D. 627 against the Jewish tribe of the Banu Qurayza. It was
after this battle that Muhammad beheaded all the surviving Jewish men. Is
Osama bin Laden's global jihad against the Jews and the Crusaders his modern-day battle reenactment against the Banu Qurayza?

In 1998, Osama bin Laden declared his global jihad against the Jews
and the Crusaders (Christians). To understand his fatwa from a psychoanalytic perspective, it is helpful to explore some historical underpinnings to his
fantasy life. They tap into Islam's social memory as recorded in the Prophet
Muhammad's biography, referred to in Arabic as the *Sira*.

Several important concepts should be explored, including concubinage, dhimmitude, and polygamy and their significance in both the life of the Prophet Muhammad and that of Osama bin Laden. Just as the book *Imitatio Cristi* is important to Christianity, the Islamic counterpart of *Imitatio Muhammadi*—in which the Prophet Muhammad's life and behaviors serve as the exemplary way for a believer to conduct himself or herself—is a key element of Islam.[1]

It is not well known to those outside the Islamic faith that the Prophet Muhammad had three famous concubines. Two were Jewish—Rayhana bint Zayd and Safiya bint Huyay—and one, Maryam Qibtiya, was a Coptic Christian. These women played a central role in how Islam relates to non-Muslims of the two other Abrahamic faiths, Judaism and Christianity.

The three concubines were dhimmis from the protected, subjugated class of the People of the Book (*ahl al kitab*)—that is, Jews and Christians. Islam considers the People of the Book to have received only partial revelation, and their respective sacred scriptures pervert the true word of Allah as it was only revealed to his final prophet, Muhammad. Dhimmi status means that the Christian and Jewish communities pay a poll tax (*jizya*), which is a symbol of submission to Islam but still allows the two communities to worship and to conduct their communal affairs in a somewhat autonomous manner.[2]

As the word "dhimmi" comes from the Arabic root meaning "to blame," the social institution of dhimmitude reinforces the splitting mentality of us versus them made manifest by jihad. It provides a built-in ideological mechanism for not having to assume responsibility for one's actions; instead, the other is always already blamed.

Historically, a dhimmi, especially a Jew, was required to abide by special regulations. Even during medieval times, a dhimmi was not allowed to wear silk or ride on a horse. He could ride only a donkey and then only sidesaddle, as women do. A dhimmi home could not be more beautiful or taller than a Muslim's, and there were other, similar rules. These regulations segregated the other for the purposes of humiliation.

There is a dispute among Muslim authorities concerning two of Mohammed's three dhimmi concubines, Rayhana and Maryam, and whether they became legitimate wives of the prophet. The dispute continues to resonate with the ambiguous nuptial status of Osama bin Laden's mother. The lowly status of the concubine is identified with the Jews and the Crusaders, but some legal authorities consider that these concubines of Muhammad's attained the status of wife upon their conversion to Islam.[3] In addition, since acceptance and "freedom are directly linked to an enslaved individual's conversion to Islam, how can conversion be of one's own volition?

It has been said that unlike Judaism and Christianity, Islam was born in the full light of day, meaning that Islam's history, including its leader's concubines, has been fully documented from its inception.[4] Just as all religions, Islam is intimately tied to a sense of personal identity. Osama bin Laden harbors a fantasy of his mother, Hamida, being a concubine rather than a "real wife of the Quran." Osama bin Laden's father's name was Muhammad. Hence the figure of the Prophet Muhammad has weighed heavily in bin Laden's psyche. His sense of embattlement on behalf of his over-idealized mother facilitated a splitting mentality of us versus them—that is, Islam versus Christian America and Jewish Israel. His hatred is intimately linked to his unresolved inability to mourn the loss of his maternal fusion. The result has been bin Laden's externalization of his rage in war, which has been described as paranoia's inability to mourn.[5]

According to Islam, a husband is allowed only four wives, but he gets around this decree by divorcing the wife who occupies the fourth position, which rotates. Muhammad bin Laden also had many "temporary" wives by *Mut'ah*, which are temporary marriage contracts (though it is sometimes also referred to as *Nikah*, which is more specifically the marriage contract).[6] This kind of marriage is especially associated with the jihad. The temporary marriage is still in common practice. Bouhdiba wrote that a Muslim is essentially a Don Juan at heart and a woman taster.[7]

There is some discrepancy about Hamida bin Laden's status as a wife, similar to that of one of the Prophet Muhammad's favorite concubines, Rayhana. Osama bin Laden complained bitterly about this issue when he was in his late teens and studying English one summer at Oxford. He lamented to a female Spanish classmate that his mother was not "a proper wife of the Quran." The implication was that she was a concubine.[8]

Hamida's marriage had been arranged by her father, who was a business associate of the senior bin Laden's, during one of his business trips to Syria. She may have been purchased because she was strikingly gorgeous and bin Laden desired her immediately.[9] In addition, Hamida's father felt his daughter was too much to handle, as she liked to wear Parisian haute couture and reportedly refused to wear a burka over her Chanel suits when she traveled abroad.[10] Her father resolved the problem by getting rid of her through an arranged early marriage and packing her off to ultra-orthodox Saudi Arabia, where Muhammad bin Laden could straighten her out.

Hamida had only one son by Muhammad bin Laden so it can be assumed that Osama improved her status, at least initially. Even if bin Laden was seeking sympathy through his self-pitying comment to his Spanish classmate, his remark reveals that he identified his mother as a concubine, at least in fantasy. Concubinage (*suriya*) falls under stringent regulation. It is also directly tied to jihad: the women of the vanquished male other are the spoils of war.

A pre-Islamic Arabian custom dictated that when the Arabs' women were at risk of being captured by their enemies, they would bury them alive rather than have them become concubines for the infidels.[11] Ibn Warraq notes: "For Muslim jurists, marriage is one of two legitimate ways that a man can have relations with a woman (the other being concubinage with a slave woman)."[12] A concubine's status immediately changes upon the birth of a son with her new name, "mother of the son" (*um walad*).

While it remains unclear if Hamida was a wife or a concubine, what is certain is that she was the hated black sheep in the harem. This negative identification meshes with the negative status of the concubine, who is considered the ultimate intruder in the family, if not the anti-wife.[13] Hence the blurring of the line between wife and concubine for Hamida magnifies the degree to which she was denigrated. The fact that she was dubbed "the Slave" is of particular interest in regard to the psychodynamics of persecution.

Bin Laden, by extension, was identified with his mother's inferior status through the cruel epithet "Son of the Slave." Being scapegoated may have reinforced his tendency to split and to project his rageful feelings as well as to identify with the downtrodden.

As most honeymooners, though, Muhammad and Hamida initially hit it off. However, as the relationship deepened, unresolved conflict over aggression and rage came into focus, and the love affair could not survive the complexities of many other wives and the known rotation of women. Apparently there are contradictory reports concerning Hamida and Osama as being either the most favorite or the least favorite mother and son in the enormous bin Laden family. The contradiction further corroborates the psychodynamic of splitting and its subsequent externalization of rage.[14] We can surmise that Hamida fell from favor with Muhammad when she was sent packing into exile to a town called Tabuk, though this time without her beloved son, who was raised mostly by nurses and nannies.

Unplugged from his maternal power supply, Osama bin Laden experienced the huge trauma of abandonment and the loss of his Early Mother, which left him feeling orphaned. Only after his father's death, when Osama was ten years old, was he sent to his mother in Tabuk.

With the death of his father, the relationship among the families changed.[15] Even before his father's death, one could characterize Osama as being father-starved because of the enormous size of the family with its many half siblings. There is no way that a father could appropriately meet the emotional needs of more than fifty children. Even under normal circumstances, a Muslim father rips his son at age seven away from the mother and takes him to the mosque. This abrupt process allows for no transitional adolescent adaptation.

While Saad Al-Fagih, a Saudi dissident living in London, stated in an interview that "he [Osama] is very close to his mother," that very closeness may serve as a cover-up for his not being able to separate from her psychologically, as well as his being locked into the relationship by the denied but extreme rage that he harbors for her.[16] Moreover, Carmen bin Laden, estranged wife of Yeslam bin Laden, relates a revealing incident with her brother-in-law Osama concerning his own infant son Abdallah. Exceeding 101 degrees, the baby became dehydrated and could not take water by spoon. The baby was howling, but bin Laden would not permit anyone to give him a baby bottle because he had some dogmatic idea about using a rubber nipple.[17] It has since come to light in a Canadian documentary on an Al-Qaeda family that bin Laden also does not allow his wives, children, and those around him to have ice, cold water, or cold American soft drinks.[18] While it remains difficult to guess the exact meaning of his behaviors, it would not be far-fetched to imagine him having some kind of disturbance concerning imbibing cold liquids. At the very least, these anecdotes indicate some kind of hidden obsession with the mother's breast. This revelation further reminds us of the role of the breast as being crucial for maternal attachment and yet holding the potential for traumatic bonding linked to early developmental problems.

Like his mother, Osama would become the black sheep of the family, compounded on account of his inability to separate psychologically from his mother. And while Carmen bin Laden was quoted as saying that she did not perceive him to have been rejected by the family, she did admit that she had not seen much of the family in years.[19] It could be that she may not have known the subtleties of the blood relationships, and she denies having been an outsider herself. Even the title of her book, *Inside the Kingdom: My Life in Saudi Arabia*, implies her status as an accepted member of the Saudi group, where membership is only achieved by blood, not by marriage.

The subject of women as wives, temporary wives, and concubines also serves as an important window on how Islam relates to the other via the archetypal relationships that the Prophet Muhammad is reported to have had. Muhammad's treatment of women must reflect his early experience with his own mother, Amina, whose name means "faithful." She has been described as "the force behind Muhammad."[20] It is common knowledge that she rejected him at birth and that he was sent to a wet nurse named Thueiba, who essentially became his surrogate mother.[21] According to Ali Sina,

> It is not clear why Amina, Muhammad's biological mother, who was a
> widow and had no other children, would give away her only child to a

surrogate mother and would not take care of him herself. This was obviously a custom of the Arabs, but it makes no sense for a single mother to give away her only child and prefer complete loneliness. Customs are never stronger than motherly instinct.[22]

While Muhammad stayed with Thueiba for some time, the surrogate relationship did not last, and he "instead was placed with Halima." It is not known why. The change, however, can be said to constitute a rejection, which at the very least compounded his sense of early maternal loss.

> During the early months of a child's life the infant cannot differentiate his own identity with that of his mother. In this case Thueiba, as far as Muhammad was concerned, was his mother. This change of "mother" from Thueiba to Halima must have been a shock for the child. [And, I would hasten to add, a terrifying experience.] Today's psychologists know about the adverse effect of such change on the emotional well being of the child, but the ignorant Arabs at that time had no clue about it.[23]

There was also a question of Muhammad's emotional stability early on. The matter was reported anecdotally in Ibn Ishaq's biography, translated by W. M. Watt, as well as in A. Guillaume's translation of Ibn Ishaq, which Ali Sina quotes concerning Halima's perceptions of the child:

> His [Muhammad's friend's] father said to me, "I am afraid that this child has had a stroke, so take him back to his family before the result appears. . . . She [Muhammad's mother] asked me what happened and gave me no peace until I told her. When she asked if I feared a demon had possessed him, I replied that I did.[24]

The boy was returned to his biological mother at age five, and shortly thereafter Amina died. Two years later Abdul Muttalib, his guardian grandfather, died. Loss compounded loss. He was then entrusted to his kind but not so wealthy uncle Abu Talib. Years later, at the age of sixty-two, the Prophet Muhammad would again experience multiple losses. Within the short period of six months, his first wife, Khadija, died and then this uncle. Shortly thereafter, he began his jihad, especially against the Jews.

Apparently, Muhammad's relationship with his uncle was very close. Abu Talib's fondness for the lad equaled that of the grandfather, Abdul Muttalib. Muhammad was his uncle's shadow, sleeping by his bed, eating at his side, and accompanying him whenever he went out. This behavior signaled his deep fear of impending loss as well as a fusion. Abu Talib nurtured Muhammad throughout his childhood and continued as his protector after he became an adult.

The exact number of wives the Prophet Muhammad had is not known and remains debatable. Generally it is agreed that at the time of the prophet's death, there were nine wives who survived him. Regarding the total number of Muhammad's wives, commentators differ in their estimates. The lowest figure given is fourteen and the highest is twenty-one, but most of his biographers agree on fourteen. In any case, his harem accommodated more than a dozen wives concurrently, not including the young concubines.[25] M. W. Pickthall, however, cites the highest number at 132.[26]

Two wives, Khadija and Zaynab bint Khuzayma, preceded the prophet in death. All of his wives received the title of Mother of the Faithful.[27] Khadija was the prophet's first wife; she was fifteen years older than he. She bore all of his children save for his son Ibrahim.

After the battle of Khaybar in A.D. 629, the Prophet Muhammad took Safiya bint Huyay as a concubine. She was the daughter of a chief of the Jewish clan of Nadir. Upon accepting Islam, she seems to have become a full wife. Rayhana bint Zayd was also of the Nadir, but her story is different. Married to a man of the Bani Qurayza tribe who died a brutal death when the Muslims massacred all the Jewish tribe's men, the prophet offered to marry her. It is said that she was an exquisite beauty (as was also once said of Hamida bin Laden.)[28] However, Rayhana refused to forsake the faith of her forefathers and preferred to remain a concubine.[29] Rayhana's defiance represents the stereotype of the Jews as a stubborn people.

The Muslims have perceived the fact that the Jews by and large were unwilling to convert as a defeat for the jihad, and hence the Muslims found an alternative method to subjugate them as dhimmi. Subhash Inamdar suggests that perhaps the Prophet Muhammad turned brutally against the Jews after they refused to accept him as their prophet.[30] From the beginning, he actively courted them and borrowed many laws and customs from Judaism in order to curry their favor, hoping that the Jews would ultimately convert. This approach is very similar to that of Martin Luther, who believed that after listening to his teachings, many Jews would acknowledge the truth and accept Christianity.[31] The Muslims' program of dhimmitude arose as a negotiated settlement. Dhimmi submission and conquest are nearly synonymous with the famous Jewish concubine Rayhana as a reminder of sexual conquest.

Islam believes that all human beings are born Muslim and become unbelievers only because their parents have not raised them correctly.[32] Thus, for Islam, the concept of conversion is a misnomer with Muslims. They prefer the English term "reversion," as in a homecoming, instead.[33]

Islamic retaliation for not reverting is dhimmitude. If the unbelievers will not convert, the Muslims will subjugate them and make them pay jizya, which signals submission. For Osama bin Laden, however, dhimmitude is not an option for the Jews and Christians. Instead, he seeks to annihilate them, as he stated in his 1998 fatwa of global jihad.

Bin Laden identifies with the Prophet Muhammad as a warrior, but here, too, he goes to the extreme by embracing Islamic suicidal terrorism without the option of conversion or even reversion being offered to its targeted victims. In his later videotapes, bin Laden does offer submission to Islam as a possibility, but such was not the case prior to the September 11 attacks. Bin Laden is embattled against his family but on his mother's behalf; moreover, he wants to champion the unjust treatment and abuse that she experienced within the larger bin Laden family. Bin Laden does this by fighting her battles and splitting off his hatred of the bad Early Mother and projecting it on to Amrika and its allies.

As seen in chapter 4, Islamic suicidal terrorism is dependent upon psychic splitting, blaming, and forging an embattled mentality with the need to annihilate its enemies. Again, it perceives America and Israel as nation-states with group selves identified with Christianity and Judaism even though all three monotheisms are often referred to as the children of Abraham.[34] While it would be easy to view this conflict as sibling rivalry among these children, contemporary psychoanalysis has come to understand such rivalry as the unspoken but manifest parental battleground where a couple displaces their mutual rage on to their children, who then act out the marital strife.[35] In turn, this strife harks back to each of the respective parent's unresolved paternal and, most especially, maternal conflicts.

Bin Laden's fatwa of global jihad is important for several reasons.[36] First, he holds no legal authority to issue such a document and thus reveals his fraudulent, anti-social, grandiose, and omnipotent self. However, bin Laden also shows how Western he is (even though he purportedly hates the West) in that he depends upon its technology—computers, faxes, cell phones, video, the news media, and so forth—to spread his message in his attempts to intimidate the West. His organization, Al-Qaeda, is structured similar to a modern-day company. Peter Bergen has dubbed it Holy War, Inc.[37]

The significance of the term "Crusader" has not been fully appreciated. While it obviously refers to the Christian wars for Holy Jerusalem and the Crusader Kingdom, meaning Israel,[38] another important reference involves the retaking of Al-Andalus, which the Muslims lost in 1492. The Catholic sovereigns Ferdinand and Isabella enacted Charlemagne's fantasy of a unified Christendom as expressed by the Spanish motto: one law, one king, one faith (*un ley, un rey, un fe*).[39] The Catholic sovereigns also militarily expelled the Muslim Moors from their last stronghold, Granada in southern Spain, liberating the land from Islam as if it were the Holy Land. Ferdinand and Isabella also institutionalized ethnic cleansing (*limpieza de sangre*) through the expulsion of the Jews in that same year, 1492, and Spain became the first colonial power in the West with its discovery of the New World. Western nation-building practices inherited this regrettable model of expulsion and forced conversion, which went hand in hand with empire building.[40]

As noted in chapter 4, bin Laden and Ayman al-Zawahiri, the so-called brains behind Al-Qaeda, both have spoken explicitly about reconquering Al-Andalus. In doing so, they reveal their group's inability to mourn loss.[41] In fact, Abdallah Azzam, the second most important Muslim ideologue after Said Qutb, wrote about the Islamic responsibility to reclaim the lost territories—namely, the Muslim lands of Afghanistan, Palestine, Bukhara, and Spain. Advocating irredentism, Malise Ruthven stresses Azzam's nostalgia, which he likens to Benito Mussolini's nostalgia for ancient Rome. A rhetoric similar to that of fascism's pervades the discourse of Al-Qaeda as well.[42]

Thus, Osama bin Laden's earliest childhood experiences, especially his father Muhammad's banishment of his beloved mother, neé Hamida Alia Ghanoum, left him a quasi-orphan among his half-siblings.[43] This rejection must have increased his rage tenfold, causing him to embrace jihad all the more. An easy target for his rage would be the dhimmi, or the Jews and the Crusaders with whom he also identified (via his ridiculing nickname, Son of the Slave) but disavowed. This conflict reinforced and deepened a profound splitting. His paranoid defenses of childhood have given way to delusional, paranoid, obsessive thinking that seeks to annihilate the Christians and the Jews, who in his mind's eye are equated with the Prophet Muhammad's three famous concubines, or sex slaves—two Jews and a Coptic Christian. Trapped in the maternal fusion, bin Laden, son of the slave, externalizes and projects his rage outward, calling for jihad against the Jews and the Crusaders; hoping to regain the crown jewel of the western caliphate, Al-Andalus; and establishing a fantasized, overidealized golden age of coexistence as he seeks to reemerge in maternal bliss.

6

BEYOND TERRORISM

The Psychological Depths of Al-Qaeda

In an unpublished manuscript, Yoram Schweitzer demonstrated the Islamic suicide bomber is a tactical tool in the arsenal of the terrorist organization Al-Qaeda.[1] Bin Laden elevated the suicide attack to previously unknown heights in terrorism while also elevating routine murder-suicide to a grandiose scale also hitherto unknown in human history. How can we understand and span these two different arenas? Counterterrorism experts such as Yoram Schweitzer have viewed the suicide bomber almost pervasively as a consciously deployed entity. I do not disagree with this idea, but it does not mean—nor is it mutually exclusive with having a parallel but dissociated unconscious dimension, if you will, by force of fantasy—that they literally act out their unconscious in a concrete way. Here, the brilliant work of Abby Stein in *Prologue to Violence: Child Abuse, Dissociation, and Crime* is helpful because she explores this difficult terrain of the dissociated in violent behavior. In addition, Dan Korem's *Rage of the Random Actor* and Gavin De Becker's *The Gift of Fear* also stress that child sexual abuse pervades those who act violently.[2] Yet there are hints and traces in Schweitzer's unpublished text that indicate there is more going on behind the scenes. The jihadis speak in a kind of pantomime about their dissociated early life experiences. I call this language Desperanto, the language of no hope, which is a pun on the name of the artificial language called Esperanto, which means one who has hope. The jihadis are desperate bullies. Because they use violence, they draw upon a universal code of violence as De Becker states in his splendid book. He notes that threats are never given from a position of power and that the only kind of intimacy an assassin can attain is in the killing of his victims.[3]

I turn to Freud's metaphor of the horse and its rider. The horse is the id, which drives humans to seek pleasure; if it has complete control, it would lead to socially and morally unacceptable behavior. The rider, or the ego, must rein in the horse/id and prevent the humans from going against society's rules. However, the ego also allows the id to have its pleasure occasionally. The horse is the driving force of energy, and the rider is the controller of that energy. However, the horse does have a life of its own. There is a vast realm, which remains relatively undiscussed, of unconscious and often nonverbal behaviors that speaks volumes, as in "a picture speaks a thousand words." This paradox has served as an obstacle to understanding terrorist behavior. Just as airport security screeners must learn to read body language, we must learn to read the "emotional" body language of the suicide bomber and the havoc he or she wreaks at the attack site. Gleaning this knowledge calls for an augmented and collaborative interdisciplinary effort. Indeed, I want to revisit what Schweitzer noted about bin Laden's view of communication. As I emphasize in the following passage, the most important message is transmitted in the terrorist's body language:

> Bin Laden stressed to Zeidan his view of the role of the media and, most important, the role of satellite television stations "*that the public and the people really like, that transmit body language before spoken language. This is often the most important thing for activating the Arab street and creating pressure on governments to limit their reliance on the United States.*"[4]

What bin Laden does not know or understand is that the terrorists also speak in a nonverbal pantomime to us about their terrors. I use the word "pantomime" here in its pedestrian sense of absurdly exaggerated behavior. We see the terrorists' terrors in their nonverbal unconscious behavior and their explicit and concrete literal use of language. Terrorists don't feel their terrors; instead, they become their terrors. With regard to Islamic suicide terrorism, a pertinent Minnesota saying comes to mind: "You can put lipstick on a pig, but it's still a pig." In other words, the terrorists can try to call it *Istishhad*, or martyrdom, and even *Ars al-Shahada*, or the martyr's marriage, but suicide terrorism is still murder-suicide. A great number of body parts and the psychodynamics don't change that much. Suicide terrorism's template, murder-suicide, also occurs in domestic violence, and body parts are the hallmark of serial killers. Both suicide and murder are manifestations of traumatic bonding's maternal attachment. As we have seen, the die is cast in early childhood.

In the preceding chapters, I have described how murder-suicide is a death fusion and a nonverbal communication of traumatic attachment. I also mention that in serial killing, body parts are the psychic representation of the unintegrated picture of the Early Mother. The Ted Bundys of this world appear to be high functioning and are often described as wonderful, upstanding citizens when in fact they are poorly put together mentally. They harbor violent fantasies behind their exterior social veneers, and they routinely act out those fantasies with deadly rage. They are predators who hide behind others. The same goes for terrorists, who are often viewed by their own people as charming. It is not within the scope of this book to map out the debate that has taken place in criminology concerning unconscious dissociated behavior as psychopathology. While space does not permit an exploration of this terrain, two authors have informed my thinking on the subject—Adrian Raine and the aforementioned Abby Stein.[5] One other author whose work I became aware of while writing this book is Alex (Sandy) Pentland. His work on unconscious social signals could also be applied to the study of terrorist behavior and nonverbal communication. It could be (and probably is being) expanded beyond its currently reported use by India in capturing terrorists through cell phone transactions with the cell phone as a latent sociometer of unconscious social networking.[6]

If I were to speculate further, one could imagine that one day it will be possible to describe in computerized detail this special, untapped, nonverbal pantomimic language that terrorists speak universally. With interdisciplinary research, a lexicon, a grammar, and a course might evolve to teach counterterrorism experts how to understand the finer points of this nonverbal language. It might make the experts more aware of what they are actually dealing with—that is, a language that would describe and factor in all the senses in its multiplicity of combinations vis-à-vis the specific, culturally held ideologies of each terrorist group. They would discover the language is that of the predator who smells terror in his targeted prey. This undertaking is a big project, but there is an urgent call to begin the task of creating such a repository. Biometrics has already been engaging this aspect of terrorist behavior, but it, too, is in the rudimentary stage. Much more can and should be done. Neuroscience would enhance such a systematic inquiry of the terrorist profile and behaviors as well.

I wish to draw a parallel between play therapy for children and terrorist behavior. If one were a mental health professional specializing, for example, in play therapy for traumatized children and the therapist repeatedly saw a child take a toy car and crash it into the back of a truck, one would wonder if the child had been anally molested or raped. We must recall that all behavior is potentially meaningful, and everyone has a mother. In this era of political correctness, we forget that we are more alike than we are different. We human beings have universal needs.

I want to tease out only a few examples of potential clues from the richness of Schweitzer's analyses with the intent to broaden the current discussion about the suicide bomber. Following are some clues that suggest we are dealing with early childhood issues. Counterterrorism experts are encouraged to think outside the box. Such thinking entails moving out of one's comfort zone, for political terrorism leads to the zone of maternal attachment. The following clues might offer a few more pieces to the bigger picture puzzle.

CLUE #1: OPERATOR'S HYPNOTIC REACTION

Schweitzer points to an auto-hypnotic trance that the suicide bomber induces in himself.[7] It is well known in psychoanalysis that the underpinnings for trancelike states arise from the relationship with the Early Mother. It involves a regression. A trance never arises out of the clear blue, de novo; rather, there are chinks in the early personality's armor that facilitate going into a trance. Regarding political terrorism, there is much talk about charisma and its intoxicating tool for the recruitment and radicalization of others to the cause. While Islamic suicide terrorism is not just suicide, we do know that people who die by suicide work up to carrying out the act.[8]

A thwarted sense of belonging to a family and community can be observed in martyrdom. Just because a jihadi comes from a big family does not mean that he felt that he belonged. In other words, the bravado of the act of being a shahid should also be understood as a way in which to gain acceptance into a family. As a strategy to regain one's honor, the martyrdom act also expresses that one feels the heavy burden of being dishonored or of shame.

The "connectedness" the terrorist feels for those in his cell or group can be read literally as an attempt to rework the pathological attachment to the Early Mother. The quest for this connectedness with a terrorist group, where one tries to feel like a "brother," articulates an inability to feel effective in one's family of origin.

CLUE #2: "WE LOVE DEATH MORE THAN YOU LOVE LIFE"

As Schweitzer has noted, terrorists have declared, "We love death more than you, our oppressors, love life." This clue involves splitting the world into black and white and reflects a problem in early childhood. Think of a toddler who is bent on saying no all the time. Think of people you may know who argue every point. If you say something is white, they will say it is black even though, in fact, it is white. This classic oppositional behavior protects a fragile self from feeling untethered by maintaining an attachment through means of conflict. Because the terrorists feel dead inside and conflict is enlivening, they thrive on conflict. Denial is an attempt to control reality, and malignant pathological control is what the terrorist is all about. Further, his feelings of shame are so profound that he responds in a puffed-out manner from wounded pride, which is potentially lethal.

Think, for example, about bungee jumping. It entails a certain bravado and dramatic flair. The person may harbor a severe terror of heights and attempts to master it through jumping. It is a counter-phobia in probably the majority of cases, because it is classic risk-taking and somewhat manic behavior. Although this activity is understood to counter a phobia, it does not resolve the underlying problem. It may desensitize the jumper to a degree so that he or she can begin to master the terror, but the terror is not gone.

As Shakespeare wrote, "The lady doth protest too much." So do the terrorists. They harbor such a severe terror of death that they quite literally must send one of their own before them in order to try to get their heads around the idea of mortality. In my opinion there is misunderstanding about a psychological function of ideologies and its imagery. The ideologies function as a kind of girdle for a fragile personality that is riddled with terror. Although terrorists will try to mask their terrors through such bravado by exclaiming that they love death more than we love life, they are terrified of dying. Human emotion cannot be engineered and completely controlled. It will always give up some clues.

CLUE #3: THE ISLAMIC BOARDING SCHOOLS

In Schweitzer's earlier work, he mentions in passing the problem of indoctrinating little boys in the martyrdom ideology. Let's take, for example, the *pesantren*, which is what the Muslim schools are called in Southeast Asia. The word itself comes from *santri*, "one who learns Islamic knowledge," and literally *per-sanlri-en*, "the place where the wise men are."[9]

These schools are the home of the terrorist organization Jemmah Islamiyah. In 1972 Abu Bakar Ba'asyir and Abdullah Sungkar established an Islamic boarding school in Solo, Java—Al-Mukmin. The school, which opened with thirty students, grew rapidly, and in 1976 it moved to a four-hectare compound outside of the city. Now it has nineteen hundred students with plans to expand. The school continues to attract more pupils, and many go on to study in Egypt's Al-Azhar University or Pakistani or Saudi Arabian madrasas.[10] The school taught a hard-line and literal interpretation of Islam based on Salafi Wahhabism and the philosophies of the nineteenth-century Islamic clerics Muhammad Abdu and Muhammad Rahid Rida. The school's list of alumni reads like a who's who of Southeast Asian terrorism.[11]

The need to hate and the need to have an enemy are first learned in the home while at the mother's breast, and then they are reinforced in the school and the social environment. Indeed, there is an Arabic saying that "children are fed hatred through their mother's milk." The parochial boarding schools play a significant role in the indoctrination process of this hatred. Most parents are very poor and hand over their sons because they cannot afford to feed and clothe them. For these boys, physical hunger then literally becomes confused with emotional hunger. By not having their parents around to provide a loving environment, they must rather depend on others, who then feed them a diet of hatred of the infidel, or the other.

The same can be said in the case of Palestinian culture. The organization Palestinian Media Watch, headed by Itamar Marcus and Barbara Crook, has documented extensively the incitement to political violence instilled in Palestinian children through all facets of the media and in the schools, especially with their textbooks.[12] One of their indoctrinators' avowed objectives—to encourage Palestinian children to seek "death for Allah"—demonstrates blatant child abuse.[13]

However, counterterrorism experts unwittingly wind up colluding with the terrorists, not because they desire to do so but because they misunderstand the psychology of child development and child-rearing practices. All of this indoctrination and incitement in the boarding schools or in day schools in the Middle East, Southeast Asia, Europe, and now America occur relatively late for the child. Instead, from in utero through birth to age three is the most critical time frame for the personality's development. The black hole in the terrorist's personality occurs during this most formative time as the infant interacts in his first relationship in life—that is, with his mother—and within the nuclear family, if there is one. And in these families, the relationships become more complicated because of polygamous marriages (actually, polygyny, meaning many wives).

Counterterrorist experts are now forced to deal with the issue of child abuse because child pornography's link to terrorism has recently come to the fore. Massive volumes of child pornography have been found on captured jihadi computers. While it is not within the scope of this book to address this horrendous topic, as early as 2001, Jamie Glazov rightfully noted that behind Islamic terrorism there is sexual rage.[14] Stephen Brown has further documented the history of this perverse behavior since 9/11 vis-à-vis Islamic terrorism.[15] Baroness Neville-Jones of Great Britain, a Conservative security spokeswoman and former chairwoman of the Joint Intelligence Committee, has said: "The information about a possible link between extremism and child pornography potentially provides useful insight into three things: the methods that extremists use to communicate; the methods they use to target vulnerable people in society; and the techniques they seek to use to conceal their online activities." She added: "There is no doubt that these possible linkages should merit further research."[16]

In September 2008, in Herzliya, Israel, a colleague told me that the personnel who deal with the decryption of these computers must be given time off every three weeks because of the distressing effect of working with such psychologically toxic material.

CLUE #4: THE PROBLEM OF THE JIHADI SEEKERS AND THE INTERNET

There are many people in the world who harbor this same need to hate even though they were not raised Muslim and did not attend a pesantren or a madrasa. Nonetheless, they identify with the jihadis, and some even convert in order to act out their hatred. *Dawa*, the call to Islam, is incumbent upon every Muslim, so there is a built-in ideological mechanism to recruit—making it easier, then, to go from recruitment to radicalization.

The Internet has been dubbed the Open University of Jihad. These self-starting seekers for jihad engage in a psychological phenomenon called assortative relating. People have a tendency to form relationships based on shared interests and problems, especially where clusters of suicides are found.[17] The Internet provides a pernicious opportunity to assortatively relate.[18]

More people die by suicide per day than by lightning during an entire year. Yet we are more preoccupied with preventing the latter rather than the former. Taking precautions to prevent being struck by lightening is straight-forward too: you just get out of the weather. By contrast, it is not at all easy for people to understand how and why people die by suicide, and prevention is not clear-cut.

In the preface to his book *Man Against Himself*, Karl Menninger wrote that "to have a theory, even a false one, is better than to attribute an event to pure chance. 'Chance' explanations leave us in the dark; a theory will lead to confirmation or rejection."[19] Menninger also said that there is a little suicide and murder within each one of us. His prescience adds another dimension to this discussion.

With regard to the jihadi seekers and the Internet, factoring in the psychosexual nature of arousal and the Internet is important. While to date no one has written on the psychosexual nature of the jihadi's Internet world per se, each of us has a constellation of fantasies underpinning our conscious waking life that is uniquely idiosyncratic and can be ignited by the Internet.[20] What "turns on" one person may not "turn on" another. Within these arousal fantasies are certain imagery scenes that arouse and enliven our sense of self. It is no different for the jihadis; their fantasies are just more perverse and concrete. They mistake their thoughts for reality and act out the violent fantasies. Recall that eroticism is learned at the mother's breast. Thus, the arousal fantasies cannot be changed that much. Among consenting adults, arousal fantasies can be highly sadomasochistic, and it does not matter. And in fulfilling their fantasies, the jihad seekers do not ask for their victim's consent. That willfulness makes them not only murderers but cowards.

These four clues offer avenues for moving out of the observer's comfort zone into exploring the zone of the terrorist's early childhood, whereby it is possible to make meaning out of the seemingly senseless violence. Terrorists want us to think that their behavior can't be understood because if it is explainable, it becomes demystified. Then the proverbial "emperor's new clothes" syndrome exposes their naked shame and humiliation.

7

A POLITICAL SERIAL KILLING BY PROXY

Christian Ganczarski the Escort and the Djerba Synagogue Bombing

Islamic suicide attacks are a hybrid. The template, as we have seen, is the conjoint murder-suicide routinely found in domestic violence. The obsession with the production of body parts links suicide terrorism to serial killing. Sam Vaknin noted the parallel between the terrorist and the serial killer[1]; however, he did not draw a link to the suicide attack. As we shall see, all three are related.[2]

Christian Ganczarski is a "White Moor." North African Muslims use this slang term to describe the European Caucasian converts to Islam. Ganczarski was implicated in the suicide truck bombing of the ancient Tunisian Djerba Al-Ghriba Synagogue, which was carried out by Nizar Nawar, the suicide bomber. He and other Al-Qaeda terrorists went on trial for the bombing in January 2009.

It was the first time that a Tunisian who had trained in the Afghanistan camps struck out on his own as a "freelancer" in an Al-Qaeda-approved and financed mission. Further, it was Al-Qaeda's first strike after September 11. In the bombing, Nawar murdered twenty-one persons, fourteen of whom were German tourists, on April 11, 2002.

The Germans experienced this bombing as a wake-up call, recognizing that German Muslim Al-Qaeda terrorists lived among them and could act as the U.S. bomber Timothy McVeigh did in Oklahoma City and murder their own innocent, civilian German citizens. Moreover, it was similar to the wake-up call that the Arab Muslim world would experience in May of the following year, with the suicide attacks in Riyadh, Saudi Arabia, and Casablanca, Morocco. As noted previously, Al-Qaeda has not hesitated to kill and murder fellow Muslims worldwide, even during the month of Ramadan. Why should this transgression be surprising? In domestic violence, killing one's own family members is a common occurrence. Sectarian suicide terrorism is no different as it is a form of murder within one's extended family—that is, the nation-state.

Nawar has been described as "a 24-year-old drifter and former smuggler . . . who came from a local lower middle-class Tunisian family. He had no radical history but had spent time in Montreal, Canada, where he may have become involved in Algerian radical groups. He also had radical Muslim friends in Germany."[3] He was known to have had contact with and support from Khalid Sheikh Muhammad, the mastermind behind the September 11 attacks. The Djerba attack is one of the few times that Al-Qaeda publicly used its group name in claiming responsibility for an attack.

Nawar's helpmate, Ganczarski, had remained at large even though two different authorities—first the Germans and then the Saudis—had arrested and released him twice before. The reason given for his release was insufficient evidence. On June 2, 2002, Ganczarski was arrested again, this time in Paris at the Charles de Gaulle Airport. He "was expected to be put under investigation with one step short of being officially charged on Friday or Saturday in connection with the French investigation into the Djerba attack."[4]

Al-Qaeda always leaves its MO calling card at each of its suicide bombing sites, or crime scenes. The Tunisian bombing likewise carried a specific signature on account of its chosen target, the ancient Al-Ghriba Synagogue built in A.D. 586. To this day, the synagogue remains a place of pilgrimage for Sephardic Jews, many of whom are descendants of the Jews of Spain and Portugal who were forcibly expelled by the Catholic sovereigns Ferdinand and Isabella in 1492. Nawar could not tolerate the existence of Jews who "contaminated" his motherland, Tunisia, just as bin Laden could not tolerate the Americans' presence on Saudi soil because it contaminated his "mother," Mecca. So joining the fighting in the path of God (fi sabil Allah), Nawar set off on jihad to plot the Jews' destruction. Ironically, but nonetheless tragically, he murdered a significant number of German tourists and no Jews.

Even though Nawar was a freelancer, he was dependent upon an elaborate terrorist organization's network and all its different operatives who fulfill integral roles. The network includes the charismatic leader who keeps the group fused and mesmerized; the recruiter who targets a potential suicide bomber; the courier who carries money and messages; the handler who further indoctrinates and grooms the suicide bomber for the attack[5]; the minder who hides the explosives as well as the suicide bomber, the tactical tool in their arsenal, in a safe house; and the escort who accompanies the suicide bomber, now considered a *shahid hai* (living martyr), on his final journey. In his group, Nawar took on the shahid hai's role.

The term "escort" is routinely used in prostitution. How might the term be relevant for Al-Qaeda? Researcher Yoram Schweitzer characterizes the Al-Qaeda recruiters and handlers as terrorist "pimps." In consideration of this labeling, maybe Al-Qaeda and other Islamic terrorist groups should be thought of as a kind of religious mafia. Bearing in mind that funding for these kinds of terrorist operations is obtained routinely through illegal drug trafficking or narco-terrorism, the idea of these groups as belonging to a sectarian mafia is a valid one. In Al-Qaeda's Djerba Synagogue bombing, what role could Ganczarski have played as an operative for Nawar, the suicide truck bomber? Could he have been Nawar's handler? What is known so far is that the two men together with their terrorist, albeit religious, mafioso network were able to erase twenty-one lives in a flash.

Nawar had installed a thirteen hundred–gallon cistern on the back of a used truck that he had purchased with twenty thousand dollars Al-Qaeda had given him as seed money for the operation. He was allegedly going to use the cistern for transporting olive oil for his new business. Instead, he filled it with liquid propane in order to ensure the truck bomb's detonation and his self-immolation. Nawar's self-immolation was not a dying-without-killing as was the Buddhist monk Thich Quan Duc's protest in Saigon on June 11, 1963[6]; rather, Nawar's was a politically motivated, deliberately planned mass murder and group-assisted suicide by immolation. Nawar's explosion ripped through the courtyard and synagogue, constructing a grizzly tableau. It also constitutes a crime scene and will be treated here as such from a psychoanalytic perspective. As a mise-en-scène it reveals quite transparently the disturbed psyche of the fused group self and a perverse hyper asabiya, or the binding of a group in group solidarity that represents honor.[7] Al-Qaeda members are tightly bound together, and Ganczarski's unconscious is fused to the organization. The group's psyche shares a striking similarity to that of a regular serial killer.

As a White Moor, Ganczarski became deeply involved in radical Islam. There is a built-in irony in the term "White Moor," as the word "Moor" derives from the Greek *maurus*, meaning "black," from whence Mauritania takes its name. Race and ethnicity politics, however, are said not to be an issue in Islam, which is portrayed as a religion of tolerance, equality, and brotherhood.

Bin Laden also promotes this fictitious racial and ethnic utopia for Al-Qaeda, but the cells are predicated on ethnic differences.[8] Turning to a deposition given by Ganczarski while detained by the Germans, the question of ethnicity and race comes into better focus. Even though the deposition is not of his volition, it is nonetheless a valuable first-person narrative. He acknowledges that he received Nawar's last phone call but claims that he knew nothing about the attack. Admittedly a phone contact would not in and of itself lead to a successful legal prosecution of Ganczarski as an Al-Qaeda terrorist; nonetheless, from a psychological point of view, it reveals him as an accomplice to mass murder by proxy.

On the surface, Ganczarski looks quite normal with regard to the deposition, conforming to the idea that there is no profile for terrorists and, by extension, for suicide bombers. Many experts who have been working in the field of counterterrorism for years continue to make this claim, so there is a need for caution and respect for their firsthand knowledge. The capacity to delve into the personality by placing behaviors and fantasies under a magnifying glass, so to speak, is one advantage of psychoanalysis, where the personality is understood as arising out of early childhood experiences.

Oddly, the profilers who assert that there is no common profile for the terrorists or the suicide bombers in particular are correct if one keeps to the surface of the research material, but once one begins to look deeper, there are some dead giveaways—above all, the body parts of the crime scene at the suicide bombing attack. In 1997 Robert Robins and Jerrold Post coined the term "political paranoia" to describe the group dynamics for terrorism, and even knowing that a person's paranoia arises out of the early childhood experience with the mother, they make no mention of this fact or of how the maternal fusion precipitates an impaired sense of reality and its ramifications for political violence.[9] After all, Islamic suicide terrorism would not be the first time in human history that such group impairment has terrorized the world. The Third Reich clearly demonstrated an impaired sense of reality, raising the question of what is sane in an insane society. That question can also be translated to the family: what is sane in a paranoid family?

In their *Wall Street Journal* account of the Djerba Synagogue bombing, David Cloud and Ian Johnson wrote that Nizar Nawar was fascinated by Ibrahim, Ganczarski's chosen post-conversion Muslim name.

"Nawar was impressed with Ganczarski. He was someone different, but a Muslim," says a German intelligence official. "They shared the goal of wanting to rid the Islamic world of what they saw as Jewish intruders." Their shared object of hatred was the same—the Jew who has long been embraced in German-Arab relations as the hated other. In addition, Nawar's fascination with Ganczarski mirrors the German fascination for the noble Arab as the idealized exotic and erotic Semite versus the Semite Jew who, by now, has become villainized.[10]

The following is an excerpt translation of the deposition of the final phone call as reported by Cloud and Johnson:

"Don't forget to remember me in your prayers. Don't forget," Mr. Nawar said in Arabic in the two-minute call.

"God willing," said Mr. Ganczarski. "How are you doing? Well?"

"Good, good," Mr. Nawar replied. The transcript gives no indication that Mr. Ganczarski knew Mr. Nawar's intentions. Mr. Nawar spoke cryptically. When asked where he was, he said, "I'm outside, away."

"Aha. God willing. Do you need anything?" Mr. Ganczarski asked.

"No, thanks. I have called you . . . I need [your] blessing."

"God willing. Ok."

"Go in peace," Mr. Nawar said, finally.

"Go in peace," Mr. Ganczarski replied. "God's mercy and blessing be with you."[11]

A short time thereafter, Nawar drove his used truck, with its specially fitted and liquid propane–filled cistern, to the ancient synagogue and detonated the bomb, murdering and maiming many. Its tableau represents a political serial killing: his suicide was group assisted and accompanied by mass murder, which could not have been achieved without a group effort that was made possible by a fused group psyche. Just as in a religious mafia, these murderers rationalize their actions as justified by political oppression and sanctified by religious conviction.

8

HOW CAN WE STOP ISLAMIC SUICIDE TERRORISM?

While writing this book, I have been repeatedly asked what can be done to stop Islamic suicide terrorism. At first the answer seemed so obvious: treat all Muslim women, and especially little girls, better. Moreover, as a psychoanalyst, I am trained to be reflective and not to advise patients what to do, save for when the issue of abuse arises. In that case, then, it is imperative that as an analyst I be forthcoming in what needs to be done because the patient's impairment, caused by splitting and blaming, yields a distorted view of reality. The psychoanalyst must explore the options available with the patient to stop the abuse. The thrust of the analyst's work is not so much to state what needs to be done but instead what stands in the way of the patient's distorted mind coming to the most obvious realization.

In all my research, I realized that answering the question of what *must* we do to stop this kind of terrorism had left me feeling numb, overwhelmed, paralyzed. After all, doesn't writing a book that explains the psychological meaning and dynamics of how Islamic suicide attacks work qualify as having done enough? Hasn't it been enough to fend off the slings and arrows of nay-sayers who pooh-poohed my theory about the Early Mother? Even my colleague Yoram Schweitzer, who informally recruited me to the study of terrorism before 9/11, dubbed my theory the Mother's Sour Milk theory. Others blindsided me frequently with snide remarks at conferences after my presentations. I then realized that these jibes were backhanded compliments and grist for the analytic mill. They were communicating to me that I had taken them outside their comfort zone and that they felt terrified but didn't know it.

Then one day I read about Somali culture because I wanted to understand the Somali diaspora in Minnesota, which has the largest population of Somalis outside of Mogadishu. I discovered that the etymology of the word "Somalia" is *Somaal*, which means either "go milk the camel" or "milk." The proverbial light went on. In that part of the world, deprivation is huge. Camel's milk is crucial for existence. It is naive to think that a devalued female, growing up in a culture under such adverse conditions and where female genital mutilation takes place, can later mother in a relaxed manner and make a "motherboard" for the baby's mind. While this material may be very sensitive to discuss from the point of view of political correctness, to understand this population's risk of radicalization and political violence, the quality of maternal attachment needs to be factored into the debate.

My questioners' feeling of helplessness—their expressions of not being able to do anything to stop suicide terrorism—is exactly the desired response these terrorists are looking for. In eliciting it, they can make us submit to their perverse will. They need us to feel at a complete loss with a profound sense of helplessness *and* hopelessness. In short, they want us to feel as they do. It is as if they are throwing a psychological burka over us. They lead lives devoid of any joy and are filled instead with an obsession for death. But we are not incompetent or helpless. We have options and possibilities. We must resist the paralysis and the tendency to deny their murderous intent. To stop suicide terrorism, the following must be done. The following, in fact, *can* be done.

WHAT WE CAN DO IN THE GLOBAL COMMUNITY

1. First and foremost, we must always remember that we are not hopeless

or helpless. The terrorists want us to feel this way and as if we do not have options for change. But we are *not* powerless. Indeed, we are trying to deal with the phenomena of suicide terrorism.

2. We must confront the stark reality that the political violence of Islamic suicide terrorism is directly related to domestic violence. We must face the fact that suicide terrorism is linked to domestic violence by the use of murder-suicide. We must not be in denial and recognize that the two problems go hand in hand. While domestic violence tragically happens too frequently, it does not make us observers feel helpless or hopeless though we may be apathetic. We should not be. With political terrorism, a shift occurs, making it mandatory that we deal with this unseemly violence because it destroys the cultural fabric of life. Just as domestic violence is a common occurrence in all cultures throughout the world, Islamic suicide terrorism has followed suit, and it too has gone global. By recognizing the shared commonality between domestic violence and Islamic suicide terrorism, we can draw on preexisting strategies used to fight domestic violence and screen for terrorism through all available means—medical, legal, criminal—and by communitywide efforts such as Neighborhood Watch and so on. For example, law enforcement officials who go into immigrant homes to investigate domestic violence calls have the opportunity to view what else is going on. They can observe and make note of posters of Osama bin Laden and of hate materials, for example, and they may even stumble upon bomb-making materials.

3. We must recognize that Islamic suicide terrorism's violence and hatred are misdirected against the innocent. The inappropriate murderous rage is unconsciously meant for the terrorists' *mothers*. The gender apartheid of all these male-dominated Islamic terrorist groups reveals and expresses violence against women. Such violence is always displaced violence against the perpetrator's mother from childhood. Even female suicide bombers deny their own female identity and do the bidding of their Muslim men. These women also harbor murderous rage against their own mothers. Why? Because they have internalized the

men's hatred of women as self-hatred. We must be clear, then, in setting limits. Islamic suicide terrorism is wrong. It is unacceptable. It violates *all* human norms of behavior. Therefore, we must make special and massive efforts to reeducate all people across the globe about the real roots of this violence, which begins in early childhood.

4. The little girl living in an Arab Muslim culture anywhere in the world is our most endangered human being. She must be protected from all forms of child abuse: female genital mutilation, which I call honor *soul* murder; sexual, emotional, verbal, physical, and financial abuse; and, above all, the honor killing. In addition, there should be an international ban on burkas both for security reasons and as a human rights policy. Special measures must be taken to ensure a safe and secure environment for young Muslim girls in which to grow up, because one day they will become mothers. We want them to be successful in their mothering and to feel competent and confident. They should no longer be forced to seek omnipotence and power through either producing sons or devaluing their daughters. Furthermore, their educational needs must be met. And most important, no little girl should have to live her life under the death threat of an honor killing or the threat of being coerced into becoming a female suicide bomber. No little girl should be left behind.

5. We must understand paranoia: what it is, how it works, and why paranoia's impaired thinking can lead to murder-suicide. We must not be afraid to call it as it is. We must call a delusion, a delusion and not label it merely the politically correct "subjective experience" of the other. We all harbor paranoid ideation, but our sanity matters to what degree and how often we experience it. Even though a delusion is an attempt to fend off internal anxiety, chaos, and confusion for the Islamic terrorists, they have no right to take their murderous rage out on others. If these terrorists are caught, they must be reeducated, rehabilitated, and then monitored so that there is little opportunity to relapse. We must take an approach similar to the treatment sex offenders receive. Saudi Arabia, of all places, has introduced art therapy as a way to rehabilitate jihadis,

using the jihadis' senses to try and undo their tendency toward predator behavior. This note, however, does not mean to exclude the option of pursuing the death penalty or indefinite detention for certain terrorists.

6. We must study Islam and its ideologies, especially Shiite Islam, which fostered modern suicide terrorism. We must be honest about recognizing that Islam's thoughts, beliefs, and ideologies exacerbate the globalization of suicide terrorism because its totalitarian, authoritarian, and grandiose directives lead to polarity with the other—meaning us nonbelievers—as non-equals. Its ideologies come loaded with splitting so that it promotes and advances splitting. This defensive strategy is a key ingredient in the volatile mix, making the combination of factors—the mother factor, the unseverable bond factor, the shaming factor, and others—lead to explosive paranoia. Katharina von Kellenbach's remarks on genocide are also applicable to Islamic suicide terrorism, the primary tactical tool to eradicate the Jews and the Christians. She has written: "Genocide entraps thousands of people in webs of complicity and collusion. It is always more than the work of one dictator, one party, or even one people. Ideologies of hate and supremacy are ever powerful and persuasive, and their appeal transcends particular times and cultures. It is by listening to the drowned voices from the killing fields that we guard against the future spilling of blood of our brothers and sisters."[1] The same entrapment occurs with Islamic suicide attacks with regard to the Arab Muslim world. All we have to do is think of the ongoing genocide in Darfur, Sudan.

7. Victimhood is *not* in the "eye of the beholder" for the Islamic terrorist of suicide terrorism and for the perpetrator of domestic violence. There is no moral equivalency. Islamic suicide terrorism is not about the subjective experience concerning who is the real victim. Any journalistic or academic writing that attempts to claim that engaging in Islamic suicide terrorism or becoming a suicide bomber is "normal" must be held accountable to a standard of international ethics. After World War II, there arose the philosophical question of who was sane in an insane

society concerning Nazi Germany and fascist Japan. This question remains relevant and applicable to the Arab Muslim world with regard to Islamic suicide terrorism. Furthermore, any society that knowingly harbors suicide bombers and venerates them as well as raises them from the cradle is an accomplice to murder and massacre. The charade of moral equivalency feeds the beast of paranoia that causes wanton death and destruction without assuming responsibility for its actions.

8. We must learn to set limits, to draw boundaries, and to not be bullied into being terrified and unconsciously identifying with the Islamic terrorist-aggressors. The simple building of the security fence in Israel is a concrete representation of the residents' need to have an established boundary, just as a couple must set boundaries within their relationship. So far the fence has proved a highly successful obstacle to foiling further suicide attacks.

9. There must be an international consensus written into law that states explicitly that Islamic suicide terrorism is against all acceptable norms of human behavior. Suicide terrorism, in general, and Islamic suicide terrorism, in particular, must be outlawed and punished because it is premeditated murder. In 2004, U.S.-based Jordanian writer and researcher Dr. Shaker Al-Nabulsi penned a petition to the United Nations that was signed by moderate Muslims "to establish an international tribunal which would prosecute terrorists, as well as people and institutions, primarily religious clerics, that incite terrorism."[2] Similarly, the United Nations must be petitioned to outlaw any kind of Islamic suicide attack.

10. Massive reeducation for young Muslim girls must address issues concerning the nature of trauma, its treatments, and its impact on self-esteem and literacy. Literacy education must also include a special component concerning money and financial matters. Learning how money works and establishing that a young woman has every right to begin to acquire financial equity while living in her parents' home are safeguards against abuse. This issue is also related to the right to inherit. Thus, a massive educational effort for Muslim girls is very different from reedu-

cation under the theocracy of Islamic sharia law. Indeed, the Taliban continues to try to disrupt any kind of education for Muslim children by murdering teachers, by burning and razing schools, and by attacking students in gas and acid attacks.

11. Currently, not all children have the right to separate from his or her mother. Every child should have this human right to separate from his or her mother psychologically and emotionally. This claim must become a written international statute, spelling it out explicitly as a child's inherent right. Any culture that seeks to bind the child to its mother under the deceitful guise that it is the culture's normative practice creates intolerable violence and constitutes child abuse. To claim that the bond between mother and child is "unseverable" (as in traditional Arab Muslim cultures and Hindu culture)[3] and not to explore what that means psychologically (as if it should be considered an acceptable cultural practice that cannot and should not be questioned) are unconscionable. Furthermore, it diminishes the psychological well-being of the child and is analogous to the cultural practice of female circumcision. Culture must never provide a shield for abuse and murder. In cultures where it has been impermissible for the child to separate from the mother psychologically, this issue must be confronted, and people must be educated as to why it abuses a child's human rights. It is also a fundamentally destructive detriment to all societies because it puts the child at risk of growing up to become a suicide attacker. In addition, it perpetrates the transmission of trauma across the generations in the shame-honor clan's closed circle. Neither the public, in general, nor counterterrorism experts, in particular, have understood the psychological upshot of such an unseverable bond. It is a key contributing factor to Islamic suicide terrorism when grounded in child-rearing practices that are based on shaming.

12. Every child has the human right not to be shamed. Child-rearing practices that engage in shaming must be outlawed and specifically written into an international statute that spells out explicitly a child's inherent right to protection from abuse.

WHAT WE MUST DO IN OUR OWN COMMUNITY

Since Islamic suicide terrorism is a global problem, terrorists can find cover in the Muslim communities throughout the world. Significant Muslim communities exist in many American cities and rural areas today. Some of their members are American by birth, others are converts to Islam, and many are Muslim immigrants. We must be knowledgeable about our Muslim communities. We must learn who lives where, who does what, and how we may help them to integrate into American society.

We must also learn the names of their schools and what they mean and represent. For example, recently in St. Paul, Minnesota, it was brought to the public's attention that an Islamic charter school was named after Tariq ibn Ziyad, who invaded Spain in A.D. 711 while waging jihad. Tariq terrorized his own troops by burning his ships so that they could not escape, and they had to fight to the death. The headmaster of this federally funded Muslim charter school praised Tariq's conflagration and immolation of the fleet, but then he claimed that it was in the spirit of the Muslim leader's alleged multiculturalism in medieval Spain that the school was named after this brutal jihadi. He tried to put a good spin on the school's name by claiming that Tariq ibn Ziyad was a peacemaker, but it is not as if they named the school after Horace Mann, a leading nineteenth-century education reformer. There is also a branch in a northern suburb of the Twin Cities. Do we want a school in our midst that teaches jihad to its Muslim students by venerating the name of the jihadist who invaded the West in AD 711? There are limits to the expression of free speech.

I conclude with the above suggestions to put a stop to Islamic suicide terrorism. It is an incomplete list at best. While there is much work to be done, it is not our task to complete this work of dismantling suicide terrorism, but at the very least we must not shirk our responsibility to start the process, most especially for the next generation. By undertaking the task at hand, we move one step closer to eliminating the status quo of this murderous political violence that destroys humanity in its very essence.

NOTES

FOREWORD

1. Arno Schmitt and Jehoeda Sofer, eds., *Sexuality and Eroticism among Males in Moslem Societies* (Binghamton, NY: Harrington Park Press, 1992).

2. Ibid., 7.

3. Amnesty International, "Women in Afghanistan: The Violations Continue," June 1997, www.amnesty.org/en/library/asset/ASA11/005/1997/en/51a0c4aa-ea70-11dd-a38b-354637a2eef8/asa110051997en.html (accessed October 28, 2009); and Institute for War and Peace Reporting, "Child Sex Abuse Alarm," *Afghan Recovery Report*, February 24, 2003, www.iwpr.net/index.pl?archive/arr/arr_200302_49_eng.t (accessed May 14, 2003). See also Ghaith Abdul-Ahad, "The Dancing Boys of Afghanistan," *Guardian*, September 12, 2009, www.guardian.co.uk/world/2009/sep/12/dancing-boys-afghanistan (accessed October 28, 2009).

4. Carmen bin Laden, *Inside the Kingdom: My Life in Saudi Arabia, with Ruth Marshall* (New York: Warner Books, 2005), 179–80.

PREFACE

1. Tom Hunt, *The Cliffs of Despair: A Journey to Suicide's Edge* (New York: Random House, 2006), 187.

2. S. Rose, *The 21st-Century Brain: Explaining, Mending and Manipulating the Mind* (London: Jonathan Cape, 2005), 61.

ACKNOWLEDGMENTS

1. Stew Magnuson, "War of Words," *National Defense* 92, no. 644 (July 2007): 16.

2. Daniel Henninger, "The Blogosphere for Killers," *Wall Street Journal*, July 12, 2007, A14.

3. Benazir Bhutto, "Democracy for Pakistan," *Wall Street Journal*, June 8, 2007, A17.

1. THE MOTHER'S SHAME AND THE TERRORIST'S BLAME

1. Laurie A. Brand, "Women and the State in Jordan," in *Islam, Gender, and Social Change*, eds. Y. Yazbeck Haddad and J. L. Esposito (New York: Oxford University Press, 1998), 105.

2. J. Castelo, *The War Within* (New York: HDNet Films, Magnolia Pictures, Honet Films with Coalition Films, 2005). See also www.warwithinmovie.com (2005).

3. Tawfik Hamid, *Roots of Jihad: An Insider's View of Islamic Violence* (Top Executive Media, 2005), 18.

4. P. M. Barrett, "Trial in Idaho Will Test Antiterrorism Tactic," *Wall Street Journal*, April 12, 2004.

5. P. Chesler, "Forced Female Suicide," *Front Page Magazine*, January 22, 2004, frontpagemag.com/Articles/Read.aspx?GUID=D27D5B61-1569-452F-9C1F-488BF68C2876 (accessed June 2, 2008).

6. Howard Bloom, *The Lucifer Principle: A Scientific Expedition into the Forces of History* (New York: Atlantic Monthly Press, 1995), 243.

7. Michael P. Johnson, "Patriarchal Terrorism and Common Couple Violence: Two Forms of Violence against Women," *Journal of Marriage and Family* 57 (May 1995): 283–94.

8. Factoid in *The Week*, March 26, 2004, 16.

9. Alean l-Krenawi and John R. Graham, "Principles of Social Work Prac-

tice in the Muslim Arab World," *Arab Studies Quarterly* 25 (Fall 2003), findarticles.com/p/articles/mi_m2501/is_4_25/ai_n6129827/print.

10. S. J. Breiner, "Some Interesting Child Rearing Practices in the Arab Moslem World," in *Historical and Psychological Inquiry*, ed. Paul Elovitz (New York: International Psychohistorical Association, 1990), 121–39.

11. Ibid.

12. Vamik D. Volkan, *The Need to Have Enemies and Allies: From Clinical Practice to International Relationships* (Northvale, NJ: Jason Aronson, 1988).

13. Halim Barakat, *The Arab World: Society, Culture, and State* (Berkeley: University of California Press, 1993), 118.

14. Schmitt and Sofer, *Sexuality and Eroticism among Males*, 4.

15. Al-Turki, Thuraya, and Huda Zuraiq, "The Change of Values in the Arab Family," *The Arab Future*, October 11, 1995, 104, quoted in "Honor Killing: Killing of Women on the Basis of Family Honor," *Palestinian Human Rights Monitor* 6, no. 4 (August 2002).

16. James Richard Jewett, "Arabic Proverbs and Proverbial Phrases," *Journal of the American Oriental Society* 15 (1893): 112.

17. Abdelwahab Bouhdiba, *Sexuality in Islam*, trans. Alan Sheridan (London: Saqi Books, 1998).

18. Nancy Grace, CNN Television, November 1, 2007.

19. S. J. Breiner, *Slaughter of the Innocents: Child Abuse through the Ages and Today* (New York: Plenum Press, 1990).

20. Norman Mailer, *Ancient Evenings* (Boston: Little, Brown, 1983).

21. R. Patai, *The Arab Mind* (New York: Hatherleigh Press, 2002), quoted in Breiner, "Some Interesting Child Rearing Practices in the Arab Moslem World."

22. Allen Edwardes and Robert E. L. Masters, *The Cradle of Erotica: A Study of Afro-Asian Sexual Expression and Analysis of Erotic Freedom in Social Relationships* (New York: Julian Press, 1963), 40, 42, 239–45.

23. Bouhdiba, *Sexuality in Islam*, 165.

24. Ibid., 185.

25. Breiner, "Some Interesting Child Rearing Practices."

26. F. Sabbah, *Woman in the Muslim Unconscious* (New York: Pergamon Press, 1984).

27. Breiner, "Some Interesting Child Rearing Practices."

28. Edward Westermarck, *Ritual and Belief in Morocco* (London: Macmillan, 1926).

29. Breiner, "Some Interesting Child Rearing Practices," 121–39.

30. V. Crapanzano, "Rite of Return: Circumcision in Morocco," *Psychoanalytic Study of Society* 9 (1981): 15–36.

31. Breiner, *Slaughter of the Innocents.*

32. Sami Timimi, *Pathological Child Psychiatry and the Medicalization of Childhood* (New York: Routledge, 2002), 22.

33. Tawfik Hamid, *Inside Jihad: Understanding and Confronting Radical Islam* (self-published, 2008), 91.

2. ISLAM: IMITATION OF JUDAISM? FOOD FOR THOUGHT

1. N. Kobrin, "Moses on the Margin: A Critical Transcription and Semiotic Analysis of Eight Aljamiado-Morisco Legends of Musa" (unpublished PhD thesis, 2 vols., University of Minnesota–Minneapolis, 1984).

2. M. 'Ata ur-Rahim, *Jesus: A Prophet of Islam* (New Delhi: Nusrat Ali Nasri for Kitab Bhavan, 1992).

3. Sanhedrin 74; and personal communication with Rabbi Byron Sherwin.

4. R. Firestone, *Children of Abraham: An Introduction to Judaism for Muslims* (Hoboken, NJ: KTAV Publishing, 2001); F. E. Peters, *The Children of Abraham: Judaism, Christianity, Islam* (Princeton, NJ: Princeton University Press, 2004); and K. Durán and A. Hechiche, *Children of Abraham: An Introduction to Islam for Jews* (Hoboken, NJ: KTAV Publishing, 2001).

5. Rabbi David Polish, "Who Owns the Soul of Jerusalem?" *Reform Judaism Online*, June 2001, reformjudaismmag.net/601dp.html (accessed October 6, 2009).

6. Akbar S. Ahmed, *Islam under Siege: Living Dangerously in a Post-Honor World* (Cambridge, UK: Polity, 2003.)

7. R. Abraham, "Freud's Mother Conflict and the Formulation of the Oedipal Father," *Psychoanalytic Review* 69, no. 4 (1982): 441–53; and Avner Falk, "Political Assassination and Personality Disorder: The Cases of Lee Harvey Oswald and Yigal Amir," *Mind and Human Interaction* 12, no. 1 (2002).

8. D. Capps, *Men, Religion, and Melancholia: James, Otto, Jung, and Erikson* (New Haven: Yale University Press, 1997); and Avner Falk, *A Psychoanalytic History of the Jews* (Madison, NJ: Fairleigh Dickinson University Press, 1996).

9. S. G. Shoham, *God as the Shadow of Man: Myth and Creation* (New York: Peter Lang, 2000).

10. Falk, *A Psychoanalytic History of the Jews*, 381.

11. Thomas Patrick Hughes, *A Dictionary of Islam: Being a Cyclopaedia of the Doctrines, Rites, Ceremonies, and Customs, Together with the Technical and Theological Terms, of the Muhammadan Religion* (London: W. H. Allen, 1885), 236.

12. S. Freud, "Moses and Monotheism," in *Standard Edition of the Complete Psychological Works of Sigmund Freud*, vol. 23, *An Outline of Psycho-Analysis and Other Works*, trans. James Strachey (London: Hogarth Press and the Institute of Psychoanalysis, 1937–39), 92.

13. F. Kluge, *Etymologisches Wörterbuch der Deutschen Sprache* (Berlin, New York: de Gruyter, 1975); and N. Kobrin, "Freud's Concept of Autonomy and Strachey's Translation," *Annual of Psychoanalysis* 21 (1992): 201–23.

14. *Capitol's Concise Dictionary* (Hauppauge, NY: Barron's Educational Series, Inc., 1978), s.v. "Nachahmung"; and Polis, "Who Owns the Soul of Jerusalem?"

15. Freud, "Moses and Monotheism," 91.

16. Z. Elpeleg and S. Himmelstein, *The Grand Mufti: Haj Amin al-Hussaini, Founder of the Palestinian National Movement* (Portland, OR: Frank Cass, 1993).

17. Personal communication via e-mail with Freud Library, London, 2001.

18. H. Deutsch, "Some Forms of Emotional Disturbance and Their Relationship to Schizophrenia," *Psychoanalytic Quarterly* 11 (1934): 301–22.

19. J. E. Douglas and others, eds., *Crime Classification Manual* (New York: Lexington Books, 1992).

20. Ibid., 73.

21. Ibid., 72–73.

22. Ibid., 76.

23. Ibid., 73.

24. "Major Religions of the World Ranked by Number of Adherents," *Adherents.com: National and World Religion Statistics, Church Statistics, World Religions*, www.adherents.com/Religions_By_Adherents.html.

25. Richard B. Ullman and Doris Brothers, *The Shattered Self: A Psychoanalytic Study of Trauma* (Hillsdale, NJ: Analytic Press, 1988).

26. Ahmed, *Islam under Siege*, 168–69.

27. Bat Ye'or, *The Dhimmi: Jews and Christians under Islam*, trans. D. Maisel, P. Fenton, and D. Littman (Rutherford, NJ: Fairleigh Dickinson University Press, 1985).

28. M. Dimen, "Money, Love and Hate," *Psychoanalytic Dialogues* 4 (1994): 69–100.

29. M. Slackman, "Many in Jordan See Old Enemy in Attack: Israel," *New York Times*, November 12, 2005, A1.

30. J. H. Berke and others, eds., *Even Paranoids Have Enemies: New Perspectives in Paranoia and Persecution* (Oxfordshire, UK: Taylor & Francis, 1998).

3. THE DEATH PILOTS OF SEPTEMBER 11

1. Jason Burke, *Al-Qaeda: Casting a Shadow of Terror* (London: I. B. Tauris, 2004), 221.

2. Bouhdiba, *Sexuality in Islam*.

3. M. P. Carroll, *Catholic Cults and Devotions: A Psychological Inquiry* (Montreal: McGill-Queen's University Press, 1989), 44.

4. M. Lings, *Muhammad: His Life Based on the Earliest Sources* (New York: Inner Traditions International, 1983), 341.

5. Durán and Hechiche, *Children of Abraham.*

6. E. S. Tauber, "Symbiosis, Narcissism, Necrophilia: A Disordered Affect in the Obsessional Character," *Journal of the American Academy of Psychoanalysis* 9, no. 1 (1981): 33–49.

7. P. Waldman, "A Historian's Take on Islam Steers U.S. in Terrorism Fight," *Wall Street Journal*, February 2004.

8. M. Klein, "Notes on Some Schizoid Mechanisms," in *Developments in Psycho-Analysis*, ed. M. Klein, P. Helmann, Susan Isaacs, and J. Riviere (London: Hogarth Press, 1952), 292–320.

9. R. C. Robertiello, "Physical Techniques with Schizoid Patients," *Journal of American Academy of Psychoanalysis* 2, no. 4 (1974): 363; and J. F. Masterson, *The Narcissistic and Borderline Disorders: An Integrated Developmental Approach* (New York: Brunner/Mazel, 1981).

10. Diego Gambetta and Steffen Hertog, "Engineers of Jihad," Sociology Working Paper Number 2007-10, Department of Sociology, University of Oxford, www.nuff.ox.ac.uk/users/gambetta/Engineers%20of%20Jihad.pdf (accessed October 5, 2009).

11. Nancy Kobrin and Norman Simms, "Jihaditism? Parallels between Autism and Terrorism," *Mentalities/Mentalités* 22, no. 2 (November 2008): 1–47.

12. B. C. Meyer, "Notes on Flying and Dying," *Psychoanalytic Quarterly* 52 (1983): 327–52; E. C. Wolff, "Flying: Psychoanalytic Observations and Considerations," *Psychoanalytic Study of the Child* 37 (1982): 461–86; and A. Gordon, "Close Encounters: Unidentified Flying Object Relations," *Psychoanalytic Review* 82, no. 5 (1995): 741–51.

13. W. R. D. Fairbairn, *Psychoanalytic Studies of the Personality* (London: Tavistock Publications, 1952).

14. M. McAllister, "Mohawks and Combat Boots: The Schizoid Dilemma of Punks," *Bulletin of the Menninger Clinic* 63, no. 1 (1999): 89–102.

15. L. S. Kubie, "The Drive to Become Both Sexes," *Psychoanalytic Quarterly* 43, no. 3 (1974): 349–426.

16. S. Freud, "The Uncanny," in *Standard Edition of the Complete Psychological Works of Sigmund Freud*, vol. 17, *An Infantile Neurosis and Other*

Works, trans. James Strachey (London: Hogarth Press and the Institute of Psychoanalysis, 1917–19): 219–56.

17.   M. Fulton, personal communication with author.

18.   F. Sawyer, *The Making of the Death Pilots*, produced by J. Goetz, M. S. Singer, and C. Graeber, MSNBC Television, March 10, 2002.

19.   J. S. Goldstein, *War and Gender: How Gender Shapes the War System and Vice Versa* (Cambridge, UK: Cambridge University Press, 2001).

20.   D. Radlauer, "The Hijackings: A Pilot's View," September 13, 2001, www. ntwebweaver.com/flights.htm (accessed June 2, 2008).

21.   Jamie Glazov, "Atta's Rage Rooted in Islam's Misogyny," *FrontPageMagazine.com*, October 12, 2001, www.frontpagemag.com/readArticle. aspx?ARTID=25198 (accessed October 12, 2001).

22.   Malise Ruthven, *A Fury for God: The Islamist Attack on America* (London: Granta Books, 2002), 132.

23.   T. McDermott, *Perfect Soldiers: The Hijackers: Who They Were, Why They Did It* (New York: HarperCollins, 2005), 19.

24.   Ibid., 179.

25.   Aubrey Immelman, "Mohammed Atta's Personality," *Clio's Psyche* 8, no. 4 (2002): 185–88.

26.   J. Miller, M. Stone, and C. Mitchell, *The Cell: Inside the 9/11 Plot, and Why the FBI and CIA Failed to Stop It* (New York: Hyperion, 2003), 253.

27.   Hannah Segal, "A Note on Schizoid Mechanisms Underlying Phobia Formation," *International Journal of Psychoanalysis* 35, no. 2 (1954): 238–41.

28.   A. Hekmat, *Women and the Koran: The Status of Women in Islam* (Amherst, NY: Prometheus Books, 1997), 196.

29.   Avner Falk, "The Meaning of Jerusalem: A Psychohistorical Inquiry," *Psychohistory Review* 6, no. 1 (1987): 99–113.

30.   Howard Stein, "The Scope of Psycho-geography: The Psychoanalytic Study of Spatial Representation," *Journal of Psychoanalytic Anthropology* 7, no. 1 (1984): 23–74.

31.   Burke, *Al-Qaeda: Casting a Shadow of Terror*, 215.

32. P. L. Bergen, *Holy War, Inc.: Inside the Secret World of Osama bin Laden* (New York: Free Press, 2001), 152.

33. Sawyer, *The Making of the Death Pilots.*

34. Yoram Schweitzer and Shaul Shay, *An Expected Surprise: The September 11th Attack and Its Ramifications* [in Hebrew] (Herzliya, Israel: Mifalot Publishing, the Interdisciplinary Center, 2002).

35. Burke, *Al-Qaeda: Casting a Shadow of Terror,* 7.

36. Steve Coll, *The Bin Ladens: An Arabian Family in the American Century* (New York: Penguin Press, 2008).

37. Jacques Lacan, *Ecrits* (New York: Norton, 1966).

38. Hans Wehr, *Arabic-English Dictionary: The Hans Wehr Dictionary of Modern Written Arabic,* ed. J. M. Cowan (Ithaca, NY: Spoken Language Services, 1976).

39. Mohammed M. Haj-Yahia and R. Shor, "Battered Brides in Israeli-Arab Society," *National Council of Jewish Women Journal* 24 (2001): 3–27.

40. James Brandon and Salam Hafez, *Crimes of the Community: Honour-based Violence in the UK* (London: Centre for Social Cohesion, 2008), www.socialcohesion.co.uk/pdf/CrimesOfTheCommunity.pdf.

41. Ibid., 86.

42. I. Kershner, "The 'Martyr' Syndrome," *Jerusalem Report* 20 (October 8, 2001).

43. Ibid.

44. R. D. Laing, *The Divided Self* (New York: Pantheon Books, 1969), 115.

45. "19 Terrorists Obtained Social Security Cards," *Washington Post,* November 2, 2001.

46. F. Sawyer, *The Making of the Death Pilots,* produced by J. Goetz, M.S. Singer and C. Graeber, MSNBC Television, March 10, 2002.

47. N. Kobrin, "Islam: An Imitation of Judaism?" *Clio's Psyche* 9, no. 2 (September 2002): 61, 65–69.

48. S. L. Gilman and S. T. Katz, *Anti-Semitism in Times of Crisis* (New York: New York University Press, 1991).

49. N. Kobrin, "Das sprachproblem: kreolisierung, kulturpluralismus und

das beispiel der morisken—übersetzung—ursula link-heer," *kultuR-Revolution—zeitschrift für angewandte diskurstheorie* 10 (October 10, 1985): 63–66; and N. Kobrin, "Aljamía—Lebenstil und Gruppenbindung am Rande des christlichen," in *Europ in Stil: Geschichten und Funktionene eines kulturwissenschaftlichen Diskurselements*, eds. Hans Ulrich Gumbrecht and Ludwig Pfeiffer, trans. Ludwig Pfeiffer (Frankfurt am Main: Suhrkamp, 1986), 463–74.

50.   Gilman and Katz, *Anti-Semitism in Times of Crisis*.

51.   N. MacFarquhar, "Saturday Profile: An Unlikely Couturier from an Unlikely 'Paris,'" *New York Times*, April 27, 2002, query.nytimes.com/gst/fullpage.html?res=9E06E6DF113EF934A15757C0A9649C8B63 (accessed June 2, 2008).

52.   R. Paz, "Programmed Terrorists: An Analysis of the Letter Left behind by the September 11 Hijackers," International Institute for Counter-Terrorism (ICT), December 13, 2001.

4. OSAMA BIN LADEN: POLITICAL VIOLENCE AND ISLAMIC SUICIDAL TERRORISM

1.   Robert S. Robins and Jerrold M. Post, *Political Paranoia: The Psychopolitics of Hatred* (New Haven, CT: Yale University Press, 1997).

2.   Volkan, *The Need to Have Enemies and Allies*.

3.   H. K. Wrye, "Projections of Domestic Violence and Erotic Terror on the Film Screen," *Psychoanalytic Review* 84, no. 5 (1997): 685–86.

4.   A. Robinson, *Bin Laden: Behind the Mask of the Terrorist* (Edinburgh, UK: Mainstream Publishing, 2001), 65.

5.   Ibid., 130.

6.   Avner Falk, "Osama bin Laden and America," *Mind and Human Interaction* 12, no. 3 (2001): 169.

7.   Ruthven, *A Fury for God*, 77.

8.   M. R. Lansky, *Fathers Who Fail: Shame and Psychopathology in the Family System* (Hillsdale, NJ: Analytic Press, 1992).

9.   Haj-Yahia and Shor, "Battered Brides in Israeli-Arab Society," 3–27; M.

M. Haj-Yahia and R. Shor, "Child Maltreatment as Perceived by Arab Students of Social Science in the West Bank," *Child Abuse and Neglect: The International Journal* 19, no. 10 (1995): 1209–19; M. M. Haj-Yahia and S. Tamish, "The Rates of Child Sexual Abuse and Its Psychological Consequences as Revealed by a Study among Palestinian University Students," *Child Abuse and Neglect: The International Journal* 25, no. 10 (2001): 1303–27; and Sabbah, *Woman in the Muslim Unconscious.*

10. J. McBride, *War, Battering, and Other Sports: The Gulf between American Men and Women* (Atlantic Highlands, NJ: Humanities Press, 1995).

11. M. C. Black and M. J. Breiding, "Adverse Health Conditions and Health Risk Behaviors Associated with Intimate Partner Violence—United States, 2005," *MMWR Weekly* 57, no. 5 (February 8, 2008): 113–17, www.cdc.gov/mmwR/preview/mmwrhtml/mm5705a1.htm.

12. I. Alon, I. Gruenwald, and I. Singer, eds., *Israel Oriental Studies* XIV (New York: E. J. Brill, 1994), 246.

13. Robert A. Pape, *Dying to Win: The Strategic Logic of Suicide Terrorism* (New York: Random House, 2005); and Scott Atran, "The Genesis of Suicide Terrorism," *Science* 299 (March 7, 2003): 1534–39.

14. Barbara Victor, *Army of Roses: Inside the World of Palestinian Women Suicide Bombers* (Emmaus, PA: Rodale, 2003).

15. Robins and Post, *Political Paranoia.*

16. Joan Lachkar, "The Arab-Israeli Conflict: A Psychoanalytic Perspective" (PhD thesis, International University–Los Angeles, 1983).

17. Vamik D. Volkan and R. T. Corney, "Some Considerations of Satellite States and Satellite Dreams," *British Journal of Medical Psychology* 41 (1968): 282–90; and Volkan, *The Need to Have Enemies and Allies.*

18. Falk, *A Psychoanalytic History of the Jews*; and A. Falk, *Fratricide in the Holy Land: A Psychoanalytic View of the Arab-Israeli Conflict* (Madison: University of Wisconsin Press, 2004).

19. Joan Lachkar, "The Psychological Make-up of the Suicide Bomber," *Journal of Psychohistory* 29, no. 4 (2002): 349–67.

20. Melanie Klein, *The Writings of Melanie Klein* (New York: Free Press, 1984).

21. A. Goldberg, *The Problem of Perversion: The View from Self Psychology* (New Haven, CT: Yale University Press, 1995).

22. Anonymous Homeland Security official, Rand Counterterrorism Conference, Santa Monica, California, May 8, 2008.

23. M. Gorkin and R. Othman, *Three Mothers, Three Daughters: Palestinian Women's Stories* (Berkeley: University of California Press, 1996), 46.

24. Barakat, *The Arab World*, 118.

25. Judith Herman, *Trauma and Recovery: The Aftermath of Violence—from Domestic Abuse to Political Terror* (New York: Basic Books, 1992), 7–8.

26. Frans De Waal, *Our Inner Ape: A Leading Primatologist Explains Why We Are Who We Are* (New York: Riverhead Books, 2005).

27. Joan Lachkar, *Many Faces of Abuse: Treating the Emotional Abuse of High-Functioning Women* (Northvale, NJ: Jason Aronson, 1998).

28. James Bennet, "Between Two Homes and Two Peoples: A Soldier Wanders," *New York Times*, November 9, 2003.

29. Lachkar, "The Psychological Make-up of the Suicide Bomber," 349–67.

30. M. Momen, *An Introduction to Shi'i Islam* (New Haven: Yale University Press, 1985), 39.

31. Robinson, *Bin Laden*, 49–51.

32. N. H. Kobrin, "A Psychoanalytic Approach to bin Laden, Political Violence, and Islamic Suicidal Terrorism," *Clio's Psyche* 8, no. 4 (2002): 181–83; and N. H. Kobrin, "A Selected Bibliography on Suicidal Terrorism," *Clio's Psyche* 8, no. 4 (2002): 189–94.

33. S. Sachs, "A Nation Challenged: The Videotape; bin Laden Images Mesmerize Muslims," *New York Times*, October 9, 2001, B6.

34. S. Trifkovic, *The Sword of the Prophet: Islam: History, Theology, Impact on the World* (Boston: Regina Orthodox Press, 2002).

35. A. Falk, "Unconscious Aspects of the Arab-Israeli Conflict," *Psychoanalytic Study of Society* 17 (1992): 213–47.

36. Akbar S. Ahmed, *Discovering Islam: Making Sense of Muslim History and Society* (New York: Routledge, 1988).

37. McDermott, *Perfect Soldiers: The Hijackers*, 250.

38. M. Wangh, "The 'Evocation of a Proxy,'" *Psychoanalytic Study of the Child* 7 (1962): 451–72.

39. Anna Freud, *The Ego and the Mechanisms of Defense* (New York: International Universities Press, 1936), 132–46.

40. Falk, "Political Assassination and Personality Disorder," 2–34.

41. M. Klein, "Mourning and Its Relation to Manic States," in *Contributions to Psycho-Analysis, 1921–1945*, ed. M. Klein (London: Hogarth Press, 1948); J. Bowlby, *Attachment and Loss* (New York: Basic Books, 1969); and T. B. Brazelton, A. Bergman, and J. Simo, *Simbiosis, Individuación y Creación del Objeto* (México, D.F., México: Instituto de Investigación en Psicología Clínica y Social, A.C., 1991).

42. Lansky, *Fathers Who Fail*; and Wrye, "Projections of Domestic Violence," 685–86.

43. Haj-Yahia and Shor, "Battered Brides in Israeli-Arab Society," 27.

44. R. Spencer, *Islam Unveiled: Disturbing Questions about the World's Fastest-Growing Faith* (San Francisco: Encounter Books, 2002), 73–79.

45. Hughes, *A Dictionary of Islam*.

46. Mohammed M. Hafez, *Why Muslims Rebel: Repression and Resistance in the Islamic World* (Boulder, CO: Lynne Rienner, 2003); and Mohammed M. Hafez, *Manufacturing Human Bombs: The Making of Palestinian Suicide Bombers* (Washington, D.C.: United States Institute of Peace, 2006).

47. N. Kobrin, "The BAD Boy Bombings of Bangalore, Ahmadabad and Delhi 2008 (Postcard from America)," *Anil Aggrawal's Internet Journal of Forensic Medicine and Toxicology* 10, no. 1 (January–June 2009; published January 1, 2009), www.geradts.com/anil/ij/vol_010_no_001/others/america/letter.html (accessed: October 14, 2008).

48. R. Wright, "Since 2001, a Dramatic Increase in Suicide Bombing," *Washington Post*, April 18, 2008, www.washingtonpost.com/wp-dyn/content/article/2008/04/17/AR2008041703595.html (accessed April 18, 2008).

49. K. Ablow, *Inside the Mind of Scott Peterson* (New York: St. Martin's Press, 2005).

50. Anat Berko, *The Path to Paradise: The Inner World of Suicide Bombers and Their Dispatchers*, trans. Elizabeth Yuval (Tel Aviv: Yedioth Ahronoth Press, 2007; Westport, CT: Praeger Security International, 2007; paper, Washington, DC: Potomac Books, 2009).

5. BIN LADEN'S CONCUBINES: THE JEWS AND THE CRUSADERS?

1. Malise Ruthven, *Islam: A Very Short Introduction* (New York: Oxford University Press, 2000).

2. Bat Ye'or, *Islam and Dhimmitude: Where Civilizations Collide*, trans. M. Kochan and D. Littman (Madison, NJ: Fairleigh Dickinson University Press, 2001).

3. R. W. Maqsood, *A Basic Dictionary of Islam* (New Delhi: Goodword Books, 2001).

4. B. Lewis, "License to Kill: Usama bin Ladin's Declaration of Jihad," *Foreign Affairs* 77, no. 6 (1998): 14–19.

5. F. Fornari, *The Psychoanalysis of War, trans. Alenka Pfeifer* (Bloomington: Indiana University Press, 1974).

6. R. Gunaratna, *Inside Al Qaeda: Global Network of Terror* (New York: Columbia University Press, 2002).

7. Bouhdiba, *Sexuality in Islam*.

8. J. Muñoz, "El Chico del círculo," *El Correo*, October 10, 2001.

9. Falk, "Osama bin Laden and America," 161–72.

10. M. A. Weaver, "The Real bin Laden," *New Yorker*, January 24, 2000.

11. M. Al Fadhal, "Violation of Women's Rights in Iraq," unpublished ms. (Ljubljana, 2003).

12. Ibn Warraq, *Why I Am Not a Muslim* (Amherst, NY: Prometheus Books, 1995), 302.

13. Bouhdiba, *Sexuality in Islam*.

14. Rex A. Hudson, *Who Becomes a Terrorist and Why: The 1999 Government Report on Profiling Terrorists* (Guilford, CT: Lyons Press, 2002), 171.

15. P. A. Olsson, *Malignant Pied Pipers of Our Time: A Psychological Study of Destructive Cult Leaders from Rev. Jim Jones to Osama bin Laden* (Bal-

timore: PublishAmerica, 2005), 138. See also Robinson, *Bin Laden*.

16. J. Mayer, "The House of Bin Laden: A Family's and a Nation's Divided Loyalties," *New Yorker*, November 12, 2001.

17. M. Simons, "What's in a Name? For a Saudi Insider, Everything," *New York Times*, February 7, 2004; and bin Laden, *Inside the Kingdom*, 105–6.

18. D. Ljunggren, "Bin Laden Kids Just Laughed at the Father of Terror," *Sydney Morning Herald*, March 6, 2004, www.smh.com.au/articles/2004/03/05/1078464644917.html?from=storyrhs (accessed June 2, 2008).

19. Mayer, "The House of Bin Laden."

20. Ali Sina, "The Force Behind Muhammad," *FaithFreedom.org*, n.d., www.faithfreedom.org/Articles/sina/10306.htm (accessed June 2, 2008).

21. Ibid., 20.

22. Ibid.

23. Ibid.

24. Ibid., quoting I. Ishaq, *The Life of Muhammad*, trans. A. Guillaume (New York: Oxford University Press, 2002), 72.

25. Hekmat, *Women and the Koran*, 33–34.

26. M. W. Pickthall, *The Life of the Prophet Muhammad: A Brief History* (Beltsville, MD: Amana, 1998), 792.

27. Maqsood, *A Basic Dictionary of Islam*.

28. Robinson, *Bin Laden*, 39.

29. Hughes, *A Dictionary of Islam*, 532.

30. Subhash C. Inamdar, *Muhammad and the Rise of Islam: The Creation of Group Identity* (Madison, CT: Psychosocial Press, 2001).

31. *Encyclopedia Judaica* (New York: Macmillan, 1972), s.v. "M. Luther."

32. H. A. R. Gibb and J. H. Kramers, eds., *Concise Encyclopedia of Islam* (Boston: Brill Academic, 2001), 108.

33. Jerry S. Piven, Chris Boyd, and Henry W. Lawton, eds., *Jihad and Sacred Vengeance*, vol. 3, *Psychological Undercurrents of History* (New York: Writers' Club Press, 2002).

34. N. H. Kobrin, "Islam: An Imitation of Judaism?" *Clio's Psyche* 9, no. 2 (2002): 61, 65–69.

35. L. I. Ascherman and E. J. Safier, "Sibling Incest: A Consequence of the Individual and Family Dysfunction," *Bulletin of the Menninger Clinic* 54, no. 3 (1990): 311–22.

36. Sachs, "A Nation Challenged," B6.

37. Ibid.

37. Peter L. Bergen, *Holy War, Inc.: Inside the Secret World of Osama bin Laden* (New York: Free Press, 2001).

38. Amin Maalouf, *Crusades through Arab Eyes*, trans. Jon Rothschild (New York: Schocken Books, 1985); and Elie Gabriel Kobrin, "Israel and the Crusader Kingdom," unpublished paper, 2001.

39. Kobrin, "A Selected Bibliography on Suicidal Terrorism," 189–94.

40. Kobrin, "Moses on the Margin"; N. Kobrin, "Das sprachproblem: Kreolisierung, kulturpluralismus und das beispiel der morisken—übersetzung—Ursula link-heer," *kultuRRevolution: zeitschrift für angewandte diskurstheorie, fata morgana multikultur*, October 10, 1985, 63–66; N. Kobrin, "Aljamía—Lebenstil und Gruppenbindung am Rande des christlichen," in *Europ in Stil: Geschichten und Funktionen eines kulturwissenschaftlichen Diskurselements*, eds. Hans Ulrich Gumbrecht and Ludwig Pfeiffer, trans. Ludwig Pfeiffer (Frankfurt am Main: Suhrkamp, 1986), 463–74; A. H. Cutler and H. E. Cutler, *The Jew as Ally of the Muslim: Medieval Roots of Anti-Semitism* (Notre Dame, IN: University of Notre Dame Press, 1986); and A. W. Marx, *Faith in Nation: Exclusionary Origins in Nationalism* (Oxford, UK: Oxford University Press, 2003).

41. Ahmed, *Discovering Islam*.

42. Ruthven, *A Fury for God*.

43. Burke, *Al-Qaeda: Casting a Shadow of Terror*, 43–44.

6. BEYOND TERRORISM: THE PSYCHOLOGICAL DEPTHS OF AL-QAEDA

1. Yoram Schweitzer, "We Love Death More Than You, Our Opponents,

Love Life" (unpublished manuscript, 2009). This manuscript is an updated and revised version of a chapter titled "Al Qaeda and the Global Epidemic of Suicide Attacks," originally published in *Root Causes of Suicide Terrorism: The Globalization of Martyrdom*, ed. Ami Pedazhur (New York: Routledge, 2006).

2. Abby Stein, *Prologue to Violence: Child Abuse, Dissociation, and Crime* (New York: The Analytic Press, 2006); Dan Korem, *Rage of the Random Actor: Disarming Catastrophic Acts and Restoring Lives* (Richardson, TX: International Focus Press, 2005); and Gavin De Becker, *The Gift of Fear: Survival Signals That Protect Us from Violence* (New York: Little, Brown, 1997).

3. De Becker, *The Gift of Fear*.

4. Ahmed Zeidan, *Bin Laden Unmasked: Meetings Whose Publication Were Prohibited by the Taliban* (Beirut: World Book Company, 2003), 25.

5. See Adrian Raine, *The Psychopathology of Crime: Criminal Behavior as a Clinical Disorder* (San Diego: Academic Press, 1993).

6. Alex (Sandy) Pentland, *Honest Signals: How They Shape Our World*, with Tracy Heibeck (Cambridge, MA: The Bradford Book, MIT Press, 2008), 97.

7. Yoram Schweitzer, "Istishad as an Ideological and Practical Tool in the Hands of Al-Qaeda," *Journal of National Defense Studies* 6 (May 2008), 114.

8. T. Joiner, *Why People Die by Suicide* (Cambridge, MA: Harvard University Press, 2005), 20.

9. K. Petersen, "The Pesantren at Surialaya," *Saudi Aramco World*, November–December 1990, 8–15, www.saudiaramcoworld.com/issue/199006/the.pesantren.at.surialaya.htm.

10. Ibid., 12.

11. Ibid., 126.

12. Itmar Marcus and Barbara Cook, "PA Political Conclusions to the Israeli Withdrawal from the Gaza Strip," *Palestinian Media Watch*, September 1, 2005, www.pmw.org.il/murder.htm (accessed September 1, 2005).

13. I. Marcus, *"Ask for Death!" The Indoctrination of Palestinian Children to Seek Death for Allah—Shahada*, updated 2004 CD ROM, Palestinian Media Watch, Special Report 40, www.pmw.org.il/ask%20for%20death. htm#top.

14. Jamie Glazov, "The Sexual Rage behind Islamic Terror," *FrontPageMagazine.com*, October 4, 2001, www.frontpagemag.com/Articles/Printable. aspx?GUID=D40CFECB-5B2A-400C-BC31-2E9522FDBB04 (accessed October 4, 2001).

15. S. Brown, "The Depraved World of Jihadi Child Porno," *FrontPageMagazine.com*, October 24, 2008, www.frontpagemag.com/Articles/Printable.aspx?GUID=EFC10CD9-F671-40D1-AF69-0249117FCEC3 (accessed October 24, 2008).

16. "Link between Child Porno and Muslim Terrorists Discovered in Police Raid," *Jihad Watch*, October 17, 2008, www.jihadwatch.org/archives/023137.php (accessed October 17, 2008).

17. Joiner, *Why People Die by Suicide*, 25.

18. Ibid., 30–31.

19. Karl Menninger, *Man Against Himself* (New York: Harcourt, Brace, 1938), 33.

20. M. J. Bader, *Arousal: The Secret Logic of Sexual Fantasies* (New York: St. Martin's Press, 2002).

7. A POLITICAL SERIAL KILLING BY PROXY

1. Sam Vaknin, *Malignant Self Love: Narcissism Revisited*, ed. Lidija Rangelovska (Prague: Narcissus Publications, 2003). See also the work of Deborah Schurman-Kauflin on terrorist profiles and serial killers in: *Disturbed: Terrorist Behavior Profiles* (Atlanta: Violent Crimes Institute, 2008); *The New Predator: Women Who Kill* (New York: Algora Publishing, 2000); and *Vulture: Profiling Sadistic Serial Killers* (Boca Raton, FL: Universal Publishers, 2005).

2. N. Kobrin, "Putting the Um (Mother) Back into the Ummah's Suicide Attack," in *Suicide Bombers: The Psychological, Religious, and Other Imperatives*, ed. M. Sharpe, NATO Science for Peace and Security Studies

Series, E: Human and Societal Dynamics, 2005, vol. 41 (Amsterdam: IOS Press, 2008), 151–59. See also P. Chesler and N. Kobrin, "Serial Political Murder by Proxy," www.upi.com, December 3, 2005; and for the original, longer version published online, see N. Kobrin, "Political Serial Killing by Proxy: Christian Ganczarski the Chief Perpetrator, Nizar Nawar His Proxy, and the Djerba Synagogue Bombing," *Anil Aggrawal's Internet Journal of Forensics and Toxicology* 8, no. 2 (December 2007), www.geradts.com/anil/ij/vol_008_no_002/papers/paper001.html.

3. Burke, *Al-Qaeda: Casting a Shadow of Terror*, 33.

4. P. A. Souchard, "French Authorities Arrest Two Suspects in Connection with Terror Investigations," Associated Press, June 5, 2003.

5. Berko, *The Path to Paradise*.

6. M. Biggs, "Dying without Killing: Protest by Self-Immolation," in *Making Sense of Suicide Missions*, ed. D. Gambetta (Oxford, UK: Oxford University Press, 2005).

7. A. Abd Al-Fadi, *Is the Qur'an Infallible?* (Villach, Austria: Light of Life, 1990); and Ahmed, *Islam under Siege*.

8. S. Rotella, "Al Qaeda's Stealth Weapons," *Los Angeles Times*, September 20, 2003.

9. Robins and Post, *Political Paranoia*.

10. N. Kobrin, "Political Domestic Violence in Ibrahim's Family: A Psychoanalytic Perspective," in *Eroticisms: Love, Sex, and Perversion*, ed. J. Piven and C. Goldberg, *Psychological Undercurrents of History*, vol. 5 (New York: iUniverse Inc., 2003), 104–39; and David Cloud and Ian Johnson, "Hunt for al Qaeda Misses the Likes of Nizar Nawar," *Wall Street Journal*, January 22, 2002.

11. Ibid.

8. HOW CAN WE STOP ISLAMIC SUICIDE TERRORISM?

1. Katharina Von Kellenbach, "A Pilgrimage to Belarus," *Aish.com*, October 30, 2004, www.aish.com/jewishissues/jewishsociety/A_Pilgrimage_to_Belarus.asp (accessed June 2, 2008).

2. MEMRI, "The Moderate Muslim Manifesto," *www.memri.*

org, November 12, 2004, frontpagemag.com/Articles/Printable. aspx?GUID=BF6692CF-225D-4675-9457-0E0A6470900E   (accessed June 2, 2008).

3. Timimi, *Pathological Child Psychiatry and the Medicalization of Childhood*, 22.

GLOSSARY

Key: Ar. = Arabic; **Ger.** = German; **Hebr.** = Hebrew; **Lit.** = literal meaning; **Psych.** = psychological definitions, taken and adapted from Joan Lachkar's *How to Talk to a Narcissist*; and **Sp.** = Spanish.

Aar, Ar. Shame.

Abeda, Ar. Female slave, said of Osama bin Laden's mother.

Ahl al kitab, Ar. People of the Book, referring to the Jews and the Christians.

Ajam, Ar. Unintelligible; similar to the Greek notion of a babbling barbarian. Said of a language that is not Arabic and means other or the vernacular.

Al-Andalus. The Arabic name for southern Spain, which the Arabs ruled, and means the "land of the Vandals."

Al-Aqsa Martyrs' Brigade. An affiliate Palestinian terrorist organization of Yasir Arafat's Fatah. It was the first to use Palestinian female suicide bombers.

Aljamía. Old Spanish in Arabic script.

Al-Qaeda, Ar. Meaning "base"; the name of Osama bin Laden's terrorist organization whose hallmark is simultaneous suicide attacks that cause a spectacle.

The group is also known by its more complete Arabic name **Al-Qaeda al-Sulbah** (the Solid Base).

Amrika, Ar. America.

Arab, Ar. From which the word "Arabic" derives, meaning "eloquence."

Arbeen, Lit. Forty, or the Shia religious observance that occurs forty days after Ashura, which commemorates the martyrdom of Husayn bin Ali, who was beheaded. Forty days is the usual length of the mourning period in Islam.

Arous Dam, Ar. Betrothed of Blood or the Brides of Blood, a special group of Shiite Muslim women in Lebanon who are martyrs.

Ars. Ar. Wedding.

Ars al-Shahada, Ar. Martyr's marriage of the suicide bomber to Allah.

Asabiya, Ar. Bound; from the verb *asab* (to bind), meaning "group solidarity and loyalty," which informs the Arab sense of honor.

Ashura, Lit. Tenth, or the tenth day of Muharram, which commemorates the martyrdom of Husayn ibn Ali, the grandson of the Prophet Muhammad at the Battle of Karbala, October 10, 680, or 61 AH (after Hijra, the year that Muhammad and his followers immigrated to Medina).

At-targhib, Ar. Enticement.

At-tarhib, Ar. Scare tactics.

Attunement, Psych. The rhythm of the heart and soul as it blends with another person. It is the mother-infant experience in that special moment of ecstasy of togetherness—when the infant and mother are one in harmony, bliss, and synchronicity—that exists against the backdrop of dialectic tensions of the dread of separateness.

Ayb, Ar. Shame.

Bassamat al-Farah, Ar. Nuptial smile. Also, the smile of joy noted on the face of a suicide bomber before he or she commits the act.

Bint am, Ar. Cousin marriage. Bint am is the best kind of marriage in shame-

and honor-based cultures and in Arab Muslim culture. It may, however, contribute to increased rates of autism in offspring, a percentage of whom may become violent.

Borderline Personality, Psych. This personality disorder designates a defect in the maternal attachment bond as an overconcern with the other. Many have affixed the term "as-if personalities" to borderlines in reference to their tendency to subjugate or compromise themselves. They question their sense of existence, suffer from acute abandonment and persecutory anxiety, and tend to merge with others in very painful ways to achieve a sense of bonding. Under close scrutiny and stress, they distort, misperceive, have poor impulse control, and turn suddenly against themselves and others (to attack, blame, find fault, and get even).

Burka, Ar. An enveloping outer garment some Islamic women wear to cloak the entire body.

Caliphate. From the Arabic *khilafa*, the first form of government inspired by Islam and a key concept of political Islam. Bin Laden seeks to reestablish a worldwide caliphate.

Dar al Harb, Ar. Literally meaning "House of the Sword"; also, House or Territory of War. Islam is to fight the Land or Domain of War and ultimately conquer it by jihad.

Dar al Islam, Ar. House of Islam, where Islam rules.

Dawa, Ar. Calling, as in proselytizing.

Dhimmi, Ar. From the root meaning "to blame." The term especially pertains to the Christians and the Jews who remain a subjugated class under Islamic law.

Ego, Psych. Part of an intrapsychic system responsible for functioning—that is, thinking, reality testing, judgment. The mediator between the id and superego, the ego's function is to observe the external world and preserve a true picture by eliminating old memory traces left by early impressions and perceptions.

Envy, Psych. Melanie Klein distinguishes between envy and jealousy: envy is a part-object function that is not based on love. She considers envy to be the most primitive and fundamental emotion. It exhausts external objects and is destructive in nature. Possessive and controlling, it does not allow outsiders in.

FATA. The Federal Administrative Tribal Areas that are bordered by Afghanistan to the west, with the border marked by the Durand Line; the North-West Frontier Province and the Punjab to the east; and Balochistan to the south. Bin Laden is said to be hiding in these areas.

Fatwa, Ar. A legal ruling in Islam issued by a caliph, a mufti, or a *qadi* (judge).

Fi sabil Allah, Ar. Literally, on the path of Allah and is often translated as fighting or waging jihad.

Fitra, Ar. Belief.

Geder Ha-frada, Hebr. The fence of separation Israel built in order to stop suicide bombing. It is a good example of how a concrete structure had to be instituted to limit the aberrant, aggressive, and destructive behavior of suicide bombing.

Guilt, Psych. A higher form of development than shame, it has an internal punishing voice that operates at the level of the superego—that is, an internalized, punitive, harsh parental figure. There are two kinds of guilt—valid guilt and invalid guilt. Valid guilt occurs when the person should feel guilty. Invalid guilt comes from a punitive and persecutory superego.

Hadith, (pl.) **Ahadith**, Ar. Sacred traditions; also meaning "legends," or stories that supplement the Quran, many of which are attributed to the Prophet Muhammad.

Haj, Ar. Setting out. Also the name of the pilgrimage to Mecca that is required of all Muslims.

Halal, Ar. Lawful; said especially of the dietary laws.

Hamas, Ar. Abbreviation for Harakat al-Muqaqamat al-Islamiyah (the Islamic Resistance Movement). The Palestinian terrorist organization seeks the destruction of Israel. Founded by Sheikh Yassin in 1987, it is headquartered in Gaza and heavily involved in suicide terrorism.

Hammam, Ar. Literally meaning "heat," it is a Middle East or Turkish steam bath.

Hezbollah, Ar. Party of God, or the Shiite Lebanese–based and Iranian-supported terrorist organization that introduced the concept of Islamic suicide terrorism as early as 1983. Its foundational narrative is the martyrdom of Husayn ibn Ali, who died on the plains of Karbala.

Ibn al abeda, Ar. Son of a slave. Also the derisive nickname given to Osama bin Laden by his siblings.

Id, Psych. The part of the mind in which innate, instinctual impulses and primary processes are manifest and identified with the unconscious as opposed to the ego and the superego.

Internal Objects, Psych. An intrapsychic process whereby unconscious fantasies that are felt to be persecutory, threatening, or dangerous are denounced, split off, and projected. Internal objects emanate from the part of the ego that has been introjected. Klein believed that the infant internalizes good "objects" or the "good breast." However, if the infant perceives the world as bad and dangerous, the infant internalizes the "bad breast."

Ird, Ar. Female, life-giving pelvis, which signifies female honor.

Islam, Ar. Submission to God.

Istishhad, Ar. The concept of self-sacrifice and its Istishhadiya, or martyrdom.

Jealousy, Psych. A higher form of development than envy, it is a whole-object relationship whereby one desires the object (mother) but does not seek to destroy it or the Oedipal rival (father and siblings, or those who take mother away). Jealousy, unlike envy, is a triangular relationship based on love, wherein one desires to be part of or included in the group, family, clan, or nation.

Jemaah Islamiyah. An Islamic extremist group in Indonesia.

Jihad, Ar. An effort or a striving. Also known as holy war.

Jinn, Ar. A spirit that appears in human form and carries out the wishes of its summoner. It is the basis for the English genie.

Jizya, Ar. A poll tax that is paid by the Christians and the Jews, or the People of the Book.

Kafir, Ar. Infidel, or nonbeliever.

Karbala. The city in Iraq upon whose plains Husayn ibn Ali was martyred during battle.

Khatan, Ar. Bridegroom.

Khitana. Circumcision.

Kiddush Ha-Shem, Hebr. Literally means sanctification of the Name—that is, God—and in Judaism means "martyrdom."

Limpieza de la sangre, Sp. Literally means "cleansing of blood" and is often translated as "purity of blood." It is a core concept of ethnic cleansing.

LTTE. The Liberation Tigers of Tamil Eelam in Sri Lanka, a nationalist-separatist secular terrorist organization in which 30 percent of its suicide bombers have been women. After entering negotiation talks with the Sri Lankan Sinhalese majority government for autonomous status, the LTTE laid down its arms in May 2009. While it is a secular terrorist group, the majority of its members are Hindu. The late Vellupillai Prabhakaran was their consummate placental leader as he concretized communal suicide by having all members wear necklaces bearing a cyanide capsule. Also notorious for using child soldiers.

Madina, Ar. Meaning "city" and from which derives the proper name of the holy city of Medina, in Saudi Arabia, where the Prophet Muhammad is buried.

Maternal Cameo, Psych. A new concept for suicide terrorism that gives shape to the psychological concept of the maternal fusion by using the image of a mother holding her infant, reminiscent of the Madonna with baby Jesus. Few of us like to consider the time when we were helpless infants and completely dependent on our mothers. The maternal cameo gives concrete form to the experience of the maternal symbiosis. It also replicates the terrorists' habit of engaging in concrete and transparent imitative behavior because of their inability both to separate psychologically from the maternal fusion and to mourn the loss of the Early Mother. The terrorists then are obsessed with re-creating the dyadic experience with objects, both animate and inanimate. This behavior concretely expresses their helplessness, which is experienced as terror. Those feelings then yield to murderous rage against the mother, which is displaced on to innocent victims. On a spectrum beginning with the first maternal fusion, this maternal cameo would be the prenatal mother or mother + fetus and then the mother + infant as life fusions and the murder-suicide as the death fusion.

Moor. From the Greek, meaning "dark-skinned," it is the name given to non-Arab Muslims from North Africa who converted to Islam.

Moro, Sp. Moor, referring to Berbers from North Africa. Also used in the phrase "Filipino Moro," it refers to a Muslim from the Philippines who would fight to the death.

Mufti, Ar. Religious authority concerning sharia, or Islamic, law.

Muhandis, Ar. Engineer.

Muharram, Ar. Also spelled Moharram, it is the first month of the Islamic calendar. It is also the commemoration of the martyrdom of Husayn ibn Ali (see also *Ashura*).

Mujahid, (pl.) **Mujahideen**, Ar. One who wages jihad, or a Muslim guerrilla fighter.

Mut'ah, Ar. Usufruct, or enjoyment. Also means "temporary wife" or "temporary marriage."

Nachahmung, Ger. Imitation.

Object Relations, Psych. A theory of unconscious, internal object relations in a dynamic interplay with current interpersonal experience. Based on how one relates and interacts with others in the external world, it is an approach to understanding intrapsychic and internal conflict, including the patient's projections, introjections, fantasies, distortions, delusions, and split-off aspects of the self. Klein developed the idea of the pathological splitting of "good" and "bad" objects through the defensive process of projection and introjection in relation to primitive anxiety and the death instinct (based on biology). Object relations is a powerful theory that examines unconscious fantasies and motivations, reflecting how a person can distort reality by projecting and identifying with bad objects.

Paranoid Schizoid Position, Psych. The paranoid schizoid position is a fragmented position in which thoughts and feelings are split off and projected because the psyche cannot tolerate feelings of pain, emptiness, loneliness, rejection, humiliation, or ambiguity. Klein viewed this position as the earliest phase of development, or part-object functioning, and the beginning of the primitive superego (undeveloped). On the one hand, if the child views the mother as a "good breast," the child will maintain good, warm, and hopeful feelings about the environment. On the other hand, if the infant experiences the mother as a "bad breast," the child is more likely to experience the environment as bad, attacking, and persecutory. Klein, more than any of her followers, understood the primary importance of the need for the mother and the breast.

Part Objects, Psych. The first relational unit is the feeding experience with the mother and the infant's relation to the breast. Klein believed the breast is the child's first possession, but because it is so desired, it also becomes the source of the infant's envy, greed, and hatred and is therefore susceptible to the infant's fantasized attacks. The infant internalizes the mother as good or bad or, to be more specific, as a "part object" (a "good breast" or "bad breast"). As the breast is felt to embody a great part of the infant's death instinct (persecutory anxiety), it simultaneously establishes libidinal forces, giving way to the baby's first ambivalence. Thus, one part of the mother is loved and idealized while the other is destroyed by the infant's oral, anal, sadistic, or aggressive impulses. In clinical terms, Klein referred to this as pathological splitting. Here a parent is seen as a *function* for what that the parent can provide—for example, in infancy, the breast; in later life, money and material objects.

Persecutory Anxiety, Psych. The part of the psyche that threatens and terrifies a person. It relates to what Klein has referred to as the primitive superego, an undifferentiated state that continually warns the person of imminent (often unfounded) danger. Paranoid anxiety is a feature associated with the death instinct and is more persecutory in nature. Coming from the primitive superego, its anxiety is more explosive and volatile than that from the more developed superego.

Projective Identification, Psych. In this process, one splits off an unwanted aspect of the self and puts it into the object, which then identifies or overidentifies with what is being projected. In other words, the vulnerable self will respond and internalize the negative projections. With this unconscious defensive mechanism and under the influence of projective identification, one becomes vulnerable to the coercion, manipulation, or control of the person doing the projecting. It differs from projection in that projection is a one-way process whereas projective identification is a two-way process. It is an invaluable tool to help provide meaning to the meaningless by showing how people can kill and sacrifice their own people and children or become suicide bombers. The desire for revenge and to cleanse themselves of their bad parts becomes a more pervasive force than life itself.

Psychohistory, Psych. It does for the group what psychoanalysis does for the individual. It offers a broader perspective from which to view cross-cultural differences. Using psychoanalytic tools and concepts, gathering a psychohistory allows for a better understanding of individuals, nations, governments, and political events.

Qaf-ayin-dal, Ar. The root meaning "to sit," hence known as the base. It is the root for the name Al-Qaeda.

Quran (also spelled Koran), Ar. Recitation or reading of the sacred book of the Muslims and Islam revealed to the Prophet Muhammad by God through the angel Gabriel.

Salat, Ar. Prayer five times a day.

Schizoid, Psych. Denoting or having a personality type characterized by emotional aloofness, by solitary habits with a tendency to withdraw from relationships with others, and by having a preference for hard, inanimate objects such as those found in engineering tasks.

Shahada, Ar. Proclamation of faith.

Shahid, Ar. Martyr. From the plural *shuhud* or *shahid*, *shuhada* is to "present as a witness."

Shahid hai, Ar. A living martyr who has begun his suicide mission.

Shame, Psych. A matter between the person and his group or society, while guilt is primarily a matter between a person and his conscious. Shame is the defense against the humiliation of having needs that are felt to be dangerous and persecutory. Shame is associated with anticipatory anxiety and annihilation fantasies.

Sharaf, Ar. Male honor, which can be redeemed only by willfully spilling blood. Female honor, or *ird*, can never be redeemed once it is lost.

Sharia, Ar. A path to a watering hole. It now refers to the straight path of Islam, or the law.

Shi'a, Ar. Followers, as in the followers of Ali, first cousin of the Prophet Muhammad and the husband of Fatima, the Prophet Muhammad's daughter.

Sira, Ar. Going in any manner or pace, this term is the plural form of *siyar*. It is also the record of a man's actions and exploits, stories of the ancients, and most especially, the biography of the Prophet Muhammad, which is considered sacred.

Splitting, Psych. Occurs when a person can't keep two contradictory thoughts or feelings in mind at the same time. The person therefore keeps the conflicting feelings apart and focuses on just one of them.

Superego, Psych. The literature refers to different kinds of superegos. Sigmund Freud's superego concerns itself with moral judgment, or what people think. It depicts an introjected whole figure, a parental voice or image, that operates from a point of view of morality and tells the child how to follow the rules and what will happens if he or she fails. Often signified in the "dos, don'ts, oughts, and shoulds," it represents the child's compliance and conformity with strong parental figures. Freud's superego is the internalized image that continues to live inside the child, controlling or punishing. Klein's superego, meanwhile, centers on the shame and humiliation of having needs, thoughts, and feelings that are felt to be more persecutory and hostile in nature and invade the psyche as an unmentalized experience.

Sura, Ar. A chapter of the Quran.

Suriya, Ar. Concubinage.

Swat. The Swat Valley of the North-West Frontier Province of Pakistan.

Tsawm, Ar. Dawn-to-dusk fasting.

Tsedakah, Hebr. Charity.

Tsom, Hebr. Fasting from sundown to the following sundown, or twenty-five hours.

Um, Ar. Mother.

Um walad, Ar. Mother of the son.

Umma, Ar. From the word *umm*, meaning "mother"—that is, the worldwide Muslim community.

Ummi, Ar. The diminutive form of mother, or mommy.

Un ley, un rey, un fe, Sp. One law, one king, one faith; the motto of the Catholic monarchs Ferdinand and Isabella of Spain.

Urf, Ar. Traditional tribal or village law.

White Moro, Sp. A slang term for European Caucasian converts to Islam.

Whole Objects, Psych. The infant's awareness of his mother as a "whole object." As the infant matures and as verbal expression increases, he achieves more cognitive ability and acquires the capacity to love her as a separate person with distinct needs, feelings, and desires. Guilt and jealousy replace shame and envy. Ambivalence and guilt are experienced and tolerated in relation to whole objects. The child no longer seeks to destroy the object (or mother) or the Oedipal rival (father and siblings, or those who take mother away), but can begin to live amicably with them.

Zakat, Ar. The giving of alms.

BIBLIOGRAPHY

Abd Al-Fadi, A. *Is the Qur'an Infallible?* Villach, Austria: Light of Life, 1990.

Abdul-Ahad, Ghaith. "The Dancing Boys of Afghanistan." *Guardian*, September 12, 2009. www.guardian.co.uk/world/2009/sep/12/dancing-boys-afghanistan (accessed October 28, 2009).

Ablow, K. *Inside the Mind of Scott Peterson.* New York: St. Martin's Press, 2005.

Abraham, R. "Freud's Mother Conflict and the Formulation of the Oedipal Father." *Psychoanalytic Review* 69, no. 4 (1982).

Aghaie, K. S. *The Martyrs of Karbala: Shi'i Symbols and Rituals in Modern Iran.* Seattle: University of Washington Press, 2004.

Ahmed, Akbar S. *Discovering Islam: Making Sense of Muslim History and Society.* New York: Routledge, 1988.

———. *Islam under Siege: Living Dangerously in a Post-Honor World.* Cambridge, UK: Polity, 2003.

Al Jazeera. Broadcast of Osama bin Laden cassette tape, November 12, 2002.

Alon, I., I. Gruenwald, and I. Singer, eds. *Israel Oriental Studies XIV.* New York: E. J. Brill, 1994.

Amnesty International. "Women in Afghanistan: The Violations Continue," June 1997. www.amnesty.org/en/library/asset/ASA11/005/1997/en/51a0c4aa-ea70-11dd-a38b-354637a2eef8/asa110051997en.html (accessed October 28, 2009).

Ascherman, L. I., and E. J. Safier. "Sibling Incest: A Consequence of the Individual and Family Dysfunction." *Bulletin of the Menninger Clinic* 54, no. 3 (1990).

'Ata ur-Rahim, M. *Jesus: A Prophet of Islam*. New Delhi: Nusrat Ali Nasri for Kitab Bhavan, 1992.

Atran, Scott. "The Genesis of Suicide Terrorism." *Science* 299 (March 7, 2003): 1534–39.

Bader, M. J. *Arousal: The Secret Logic of Sexual Fantasies*. New York: St. Martin's Press: New York, 2002.

Barakat, Halim. *The Arab World: Society, Culture, and State*. Berkeley: University of California Press, 1993.

Barrett, P. M. "Trial in Idaho Will Test Antiterrorism Tactic." *Wall Street Journal*, April 12, 2004.

Bat Ye'or. *The Dhimmi: Jews and Christians under Islam*. Translated by D. Maisel, P. Fenton, and D. Littman. Rutherford, NJ: Fairleigh Dickinson University Press, 1985.

———. *Islam and Dhimmitude: Where Civilizations Collide*. Translated by M. Kochan and D. Littman. Madison, NJ: Fairleigh Dickinson University Press, 2001.

Bennet, James. "Between Two Homes and Two Peoples: A Soldier Wanders." *New York Times*, November 9, 2003.

Bergen, Peter L. *Holy War, Inc.: Inside the Secret World of Osama bin Laden*. New York: Free Press, 2001.

Berke, J. H., S. Pierides, A. Sabbadini, and S. Schneider, eds. *Even Paranoids Have Enemies: New Perspectives in Paranoia and Persecution*. Oxfordshire, UK: Taylor & Francis, 1998.

Berko, Anat. *The Path to Paradise: The Inner World of the Suicide Bombers and Their Dispatchers*. Translated by Elizabeth Yuval. Tel Aviv: Yedioth Ahronoth Press, 2007; and Westport, CT: Praeger Security International, 2007. Paper edition, Washington, DC: Potomac Books, Inc., 2009.

Biggs, M. "Dying without Killing: Protest by Self-Immolation." In *Making Sense of Suicide Missions*, edited by D. Gambetta. Oxford, UK: Oxford University Press, 2005.

Bin Laden, Carmen. *Inside the Kingdom: My Life in Saudi Arabia*. With Ruth Marshall. New York: Warner Books, 2005.

Bloom, Howard. *The Lucifer Principle: A Scientific Expedition into the Forces of History*. New York: Atlantic Monthly Press, 1995.

Bouhdiba, Abdelwahab. *Sexuality in Islam*. Translated by Alan Sheridan. London: Saqi Books, 1998.

Bowlby, J. *Attachment and Loss*. New York: Basic Books, 1969.

Brand, Laurie A. "Women and the State in Jordan: Inclusion or Exclusion?" In *Islam, Gender, and Social Change*, edited by Y. Yazbeck Haddad and J. L. Esposito. New York: Oxford University Press, 1998.

Brandon, James, and Salam Hafez. *Crimes of the Community: Honour-based Violence in the UK*. London: Centre for Social Cohesion, 2008.

Brazelton, T. B., A. Bergman, and J. Simo. *Simbiosis, Individuación y Creación del Objeto*. México, D.F., México: Instituto de Investigación en Psicología Clínica y Social, A.C., 1991.

Breiner, S. J. *Slaughter of the Innocents: Child Abuse through the Ages and Today*. New York: Plenum Press, 1990.

———. "Some Interesting Child Rearing Practices in the Arab Moslem World." In *Historical and Psychological Inquiry*, edited by Paul Elovitz. New York: International Psychohistorical Association, 1990.

Brown, S. "The Depraved World of Jihadi Child Porno." *FrontPageMagazine. com*, October 24, 2008. www.frontpagemag.com/Articles/Printable. aspx?GUID=EFC10CD9-F671-40D1-AF69-0249117FCEC3.

Burke, Jason. *Al-Qaeda: Casting a Shadow of Terror*. London: I. B. Tauris, 2004.

Capitol's Concise Dictionary of Seven Languages. Hauppauge, NY: Barron's Educational Series, Inc., 1978.

Capps, D. *Men, Religion, and Melancholia: James, Otto, Jung, and Erikson*. New Haven: Yale University Press, 1997.

Carroll, M. P. *Catholic Cults and Devotions: A Psychological Inquiry*. Montreal: McGill-Queen's University Press, 1989.

Castelo, J. *The War Within*. New York: HDNet Films, Magnolia Pictures, Honet Films with Coalition Films, 2005.

Chesler, P. "Forced Female Suicide." *FrontPageMagazine.com*, January 22,

2004. frontpagemag.com/Articles/Read.aspx?GUID=D27D5B61-1569-452F-9C1F-488BF68C2876 (accessed June 2, 2008).

Cloud, David, and Ian Johnson. "Hunt for al Qaeda Misses the Likes of Nizar Nawar." *Wall Street Journal*, August 20, 2002.

Coll, Steve. *The Bin Ladens: An Arabian Family in the American Century*. New York: Penguin Press, 2008.

Crapanzano, V. "Rite of Return: Circumcision in Morocco." *Psychoanalytic Study of Society* 9 (1981).

Cutler, A. H., and H. E. Cutler. *The Jew as Ally of the Muslim: Medieval Roots of Anti-Semitism*. Notre Dame, IN: University of Notre Dame Press, 1986.

De Becker, Gavin. *The Gift of Fear: Survival Signals that Protect Us from Violence*. Boston: Little, Brown, 1997.

De Waal, Frans. *Our Inner Ape: A Leading Primatologist Explains Why We Are Who We Are*. New York: Riverhead Books, 2005.

Deutsch, Helene. "Some Forms of Emotional Disturbance and Their Relationship to Schizophrenia." *Psychoanalytic Quarterly* 11 (1934).

Dimen, M. "Money, Love and Hate." *Psychoanalytic Dialogues* 4 (1994).

Douglas, J. E., A. W. Burgess, A. G. Burgess, and R. K. Ressler, eds. *The Crime Classification Manual*. New York: Lexington Books, 1992.

Durán, K., and A. Hechiche. *Children of Abraham: An Introduction to Islam for Jews*. Hoboken, NJ: KTAV Publishing House, 2001.

Edwardes, Allen, and R. E. L. Masters. *The Cradle of Erotica: A Study of Afro-Asian Sexual Expression and Analysis of Erotic Freedom in Social Relationships*. New York: Julian Press, 1963.

Elpeleg, Z., and S. Himmelstein. *The Grand Mufti: Haj Amin al-Hussaini, Founder of the Palestinian National Movement*. Portland, OR: Frank Cass, 1993.

Encyclopedia Judaica. 16 vols. New York: Macmillan, 1972.

Fadhal, M. Al. "Violation of Women's Rights in Iraq." Unpublished ms. (Ljubljana, 2003).

Fairbairn, W. R. D. *Psychoanalytic Studies of the Personality*. London: Tavistock Publications, 1952.

Falk, Avner. *Fratricide in the Holy Land: A Psychoanalytic View of the Arab-

Israeli Conflict. Madison: University of Wisconsin Press, 2004.

———. "The Meaning of Jerusalem: A Psychohistorical Inquiry." *Psychohistory Review* 16, no. 1 (1987).

———. "Osama bin Laden and America." *Mind and Human Interaction* 12, no. 3 (2001).

———. "Political Assassination and Personality Disorder: The Cases of Lee Harvey Oswald and Yigal Amir." *Mind and Human Interaction* 12, no. 1 (2002).

———. *A Psychoanalytic History of the Jews*. Madison, NJ: Fairleigh Dickinson University Press, 1996.

———. "Unconscious Aspects of the Arab-Israeli Conflict." *Psychoanalytic Study of Society* 17 (1992).

Firestone, R. *Children of Abraham: An Introduction to Judaism for Muslims*. Hoboken, NJ: KTAV Publishing, 2001.

Fornari, F. *The Psychoanalysis of War*. Translated by Alenka Pfeifer. Bloomington: Indiana University Press, 1974.

Fouda, Yousri, and Nick Fielding. *Masterminds of Terror: The Truth behind the Most Devastating Terrorist Attack the World Has Ever Seen*. New York: Arcade Publishing, 2003.

Freud, Anna. *The Ego and the Mechanisms of Defense*. New York: International Universities Press, 1936.

Freud, Sigmund. "Moses and Monotheism." In *The Standard Edition of the Complete Psychological Works of Sigmund Freud*. Vol. 23, *An Outline of Psycho-Analysis and Other Works*. Translated by James Strachey. London: Hogarth Press and the Institute of Psychoanalysis, 1937–39.

———. "The Uncanny." In *The Standard Edition of the Complete Psychological Works of Sigmund Freud*. Vol. 17, *An Infantile Neurosis and Other Works*. Translated by James Strachey. London: Hogarth Press and the Institute of Psychoanalysis, 1917–19.

Gambetta, Diego, and Steffen Hertog. "Engineers of Jihad." Sociology Working Paper Number 2007-10. Department of Sociology, University of Oxford. www.nuff.ox.ac.uk/users/gambetta/Engineers%20of%20Jihad.pdf.

Gibb, H. A. R., and J. H. Kramers, eds. *Concise Encyclopedia of Islam*. Boston: Brill Academic, 2001.

Gilman, S. L., and S. T. Katz. *Anti-Semitism in Times of Crisis*. New York: New York University Press, 1991.

Glazov, Jamie. "Atta's Rage Rooted in Islam's Misogyny." *FrontPageMagazine.com*, October 12, 2001. www.frontpagemag.com/readArticle. aspx?ARTID=25198.

———. "The Sexual Rage behind Islamic Terror." *FrontpageMagazine. com*, October 4, 2001. www.frontpagemag.com/Articles/Printable. aspx?GUID=D40CFECB-5B2A-400C-BC31-2E9522FDBB04 (accessed October 4, 2001).

Goldberg, Arnold. *The Problem of Perversion: The View from Self Psychology*. New Haven, CT: Yale University Press, 1995.

Goldstein, Joshua S. *War and Gender: How Gender Shapes the War System and Vice Versa*. Cambridge, UK: Cambridge University Press, 2001.

Gordon, A. "Close Encounters: Unidentified Flying Object Relations." *Psychoanalytic Review* 82, no. 5 (1995).

Gorkin, M., and R. Othman. *Three Mothers, Three Daughters: Palestinian Women's Stories*. Berkeley: University of California Press, 1996.

Gunaratna, Rohan. *Inside Al Qaeda: Global Network of Terror*. New York: Columbia University Press, 2002.

Hafez, Mohammed M. *Manufacturing Human Bombs: The Making of Palestinian Suicide Bombers*. Washington, D.C.: United States Institute of Peace, 2006.

———. *Why Muslims Rebel: Repression and Resistance in the Islamic World*. Boulder, CO: Lynne Rienner, 2003.

Haj-Yahia, M. M., and R. Shor. "Battered Brides in Israeli-Arab Society." *National Council of Jewish Women Journal* 24 (2001).

———. "Child Maltreatment as Perceived by Arab Students of Social Science in the West Bank." *Child Abuse and Neglect: The International Journal* 19, no. 10 (1995).

Haj-Yahia, M. M., and S. Tamish. "The Rates of Child Sexual Abuse and Its

Psychological Consequences as Revealed by a Study among Palestinian University Students." *Child Abuse and Neglect: The International Journal* 25, no. 10 (2001).

Hamid, Tawfik. *Inside Jihad: Understanding and Confronting Radical Islam.* Self-published, 2008.

———. *Roots of Jihad: An Insider's View of Islamic Violence.* Top Executive Media, 2006.

Hekmat, Anwar. *Women and the Koran: The Status of Women in Islam.* Amherst, NY: Prometheus Books, 1997.

Henninger, Daniel. "The Blogosphere for Killers." *Wall Street Journal,* July 12, 2007.

Herman, Judith. *Trauma and Recovery: The Aftermath of Violence—from Domestic Abuse to Political Terror.* New York: Basic Books, 1992.

Hoffman, Bruce. "Defending against Suicide Terrorism." Paper presented at the Rand Corporation conference, *Three Years After: The Next Steps in the War on Terror.* Washington, D.C., September 8, 2004.

"Honor Killing: Killing of Women on the Basis of Family Honor." *Palestinian Human Rights Monitor* 6, no. 4 (August 2002).

Hudson, Rex A. *Who Becomes a Terrorist and Why: The 1999 Government Report on Profiling Terrorists.* Guilford, CT: Lyons Press, 2002.

Hughes, Thomas Patrick. *A Dictionary of Islam: Being a Cyclopaedia of the Doctrines, Rites, Ceremonies, and Customs, Together with the Technical and Theological Terms of the Muhammadan Religion.* London: W. H. Allen, 1885.

Hunt, Tom. *The Cliffs of Despair: A Journey to Suicide's Edge.* New York: Random House, 2006.

Ibn Warraq. *Why I Am Not a Muslim.* Amherst, NY: Prometheus Books, 1995.

Immelman, A. "Mohammed Atta's Personality." *Clio's Psyche* 8, no. 4 (2002).

Inamdar, Subhash. C. *Muhammad and the Rise of Islam: The Creation of Group Identity.* Madison, CT: Psychosocial Press, 2001.

Institute for War and Peace Reporting. "Child Sex Abuse Alarm." *Afghan Re-*

covery Report, February 24, 2003. www.iwpr.net/index.pl?archive/arr/arr_200302_49_eng.t (accessed May 14, 2003).

Jewett, James Richard. "Arabic Proverbs and Proverbial Phrases." Journal of the American Oriental Society 15 (1893).

Johnson, Michael P. "Patriarchal Terrorism and Common Couple Violence: Two Forms of Violence against Women." Journal of Marriage and Family 57 (May 1995): 283–94.

Joiner, T. Why People Die by Suicide. Cambridge, MA: Harvard University Press, 2005.

Karr-Morse, Robin, and Meredith Wiley. Ghosts from the Nursery: Tracing the Roots of Violence. New York: Grove, 1997.

Kershner, I. "The 'Martyr' Syndrome." Jerusalem Report 20 (October 8, 2001).

Klein, Melanie. "Mourning and Its Relation to Manic States." In Contributions to Psycho-Analysis, 1921–1945, edited by M. Klein. London: Hogarth Press, 1948.

———. "Notes on Some Schizoid Mechanisms." In Developments in Psycho-Analysis, edited by M. Klein, P. Helmann, Susan Isaacs, and J. Riviere. London: Hogarth Press, 1952.

———. The Writings of Melanie Klein. New York: Free Press, 1984.

Kluge, Friedrich. Etymologisches Wörterbuch der Deutschen Sprache. Berlin, New York: de Gruyter, 1975.

Kobrin, Elie Gabriel. "Israel and the Crusader Kingdom" (unpublished paper), 2001.

Kobrin, Nancy. "Aljamía—Lebenstil und Gruppenbindung am Rande des christlichen." In Europ in Stil: Geschichten und Funktionen eines kulturwissenschaftlichen Diskurselements, edited by Hans Ulrich Gumbrecht and Ludwig Pfeiffer, translated by Ludwig Pfeiffer. Frankfurt am Main: Suhrkamp, 1986.

———. "The BAD Boy Bombings of Bangalore, Ahmadabad and Delhi 2008 (Postcard from America)." Anil Aggrawal's Internet Journal of Forensic Medicine and Toxicology 10, no. 1 (January–June 2009; published January 1, 2009). www.geradts.com/anil/ij/vol_010_no_001/others/america/letter.html (accessed October 14, 2008).

———. "Das sprachproblem: Kreolisierung, kulturpluralismus und das beispiel der morisken—übersetzung—ursula link-heer." *kultuRRevolution: —zeitschrift für angewandte diskurstheorie*, October 10, 1985.

———. "Freud's Concept of Autonomy and Strachey's Translation." *Annual of Psychoanalysis* 21 (1992).

———. "Islam: An Imitation of Judaism?" *Clio's Psyche* 9, no. 2 (September 2002).

———. "Moses on the Margin: A Critical Transcription and Semiotic Analysis of Eight Aljamiado-Morisco Legends of Musa." PhD thesis, 2 vols., University of Minnesota– Minneapolis, 1984.

———. "Political Domestic Violence in Ibrahim's Family: A Psychoanalytic Perspective." In *Eroticisms: Love, Sex, and Perversion*, edited by J. Piven, C. Boyd, and C. Goldberg. Vol. 5 of *Psychological Undercurrents of History*, 104–39. New York: iUniverse Inc., 2003.

———. "Political Serial Killing by Proxy: Christian Ganczarski the Chief Perpetrator, Nizar Nawar His Proxy, and the Djerba Synagogue Bombing." *Anil Aggrawal's Internet Journal of Forensics and Toxicology* 8, no. 2 (December 2007). www.geradts.com/anil/ij/vol_008_no_002/papers/paper001.html.

———. "A Psychoanalytic Approach to bin Laden, Political Violence, and Islamic Suicidal Terrorism." *Clio's Psyche* 8, no. 4 (2002): 181–83.

———. "Putting the Um (Mother) Back into the Ummah's Suicide Attack." In *Suicide Bombers: The Psychological, Religious, and Other Imperatives*, edited by M. Sharpe. NATO Science for Peace and Security Studies Series, E: Human and Societal Dynamics, vol. 41. Amsterdam: IOS Press, 2008.

———. "A Selected Bibliography on Suicidal Terrorism." *Clio's Psyche* 8, no. 4 (2002).

Kobrin, Nancy, and Norman Simms. "Jihaditism? Parallels between Autism and Terrorism." *Mentalities/Mentalités* 22, no. 2 (2008).

Korem, Dan. *Rage of the Random Actor: Disarming Catastrophic Acts and Restoring Lives*. Richardson, TX: International Focus Press, 2005.

Krenawi, Alean al-, and John R. Graham. "Principles of Social Work Practice in the Muslim Arab World." *Arab Studies Quarterly* 25 (Fall 2003). findarticles.com/p/articles/mi_m2501/is_4_25/ai_n6129827/print.

Kubie, L. S. "The Drive to Become Both Sexes." *Psychoanalytic Quarterly* 43, no. 3 (1974).

Lacan, Jacques. *Ecrits*. New York: Norton, 1966.

Lachkar, Joan. "The Arab-Israeli Conflict: A Psychoanalytic Perspective." PhD thesis, International University–Los Angeles, 1983.

———. *How to Talk to a Narcissist*. New York: Routledge, 2008.

———. *Many Faces of Abuse: Treating the Emotional Abuse of High-Functioning Women*. Northvale, NJ: Jason Aronson, 1998.

———. "The Psychological Make-up of the Suicide Bomber." *Journal of Psychohistory* 29, no. 4 (2002).

Laing, R. D. *The Divided Self*. New York: Pantheon Books, 1969.

Lansky, M. R. *Fathers Who Fail: Shame and Psychopathology in the Family System*. Hillsdale, NJ: Analytic Press, 1992.

Lewis, B. "License to Kill: Usama bin Ladin's Declaration of Jihad." *Foreign Affairs* 77, no. 6 (1998).

Lings, M. *Muhammad: His Life Based on the Earliest Sources*. New York: Inner Traditions International, 1983.

"Link between Child Porno and Muslim Terrorists Discovered in Police Raid." *Jihad Watch*, October 17, 2008. www.jihadwatch.org/archives/023137.php (accessed October 17, 2008).

Ljunggren, D. "Bin Laden Kids Just Laughed at the Father of Terror." *Sydney Morning Herald*, March 6, 2004. www.smh.com.au/articles/2004/03/05/1078464644917.html?from=storyrhs (accessed June 2, 2008).

Maalouf, Amin. *Crusades through Arab Eyes*. Translated by Jon Rothschild. New York: Schocken Books, 1985.

MacFarquhar, N. "Saturday Profile: An Unlikely Couturier from an Unlikely 'Paris.'" *New York Times*, April 27, 2002. query.nytimes.com/gst/fullpage.html?res=9E06E6DF113EF934A15757C0A9649C8B63 (accessed June 2, 2008).

Magnuson, Stew. "War of Words." *National Defense* 92, no. 644 (July 2007).

Mailer, Norman. *Ancient Evenings*. Boston: Little Brown, 1983.

"Major Religions of the World Ranked by Number of Adherents." *Adherents. com: National and World Religion Statistics, Church Statistics, World Religions*. www.adherents.com/Religions_By_Adherents.html.

Manji, Irshad. *The Trouble with Islam: A Muslim's Call for Reform in Her Faith*. New York: Macmillan, 2003.

Maqsood, R. W. *A Basic Dictionary of Islam*. New Delhi: Goodword Books, 2001.

Marcus, I. *"Ask for Death!" The Indoctrination of Palestinian Children to Seek Death for Allah—Shahada*. Updated 2004 CD ROM. Palestinian Media Watch Special Report 40. www.pmw.org.il/ask%20for%20death. htm#top.

Marcus, Itmar, and Barbara Cook. "PA Political Conclusions to the Israeli Withdrawal from the Gaza Strip." *Palestinian Media Watch*, September 1, 2005. www.pmw.org.il/murder.htm (accessed September 1, 2005).

Marx, A. W. *Faith in Nation: Exclusionary Origins in Nationalism*. Oxford, UK: Oxford University Press, 2003.

Masterson, J. F. *The Narcissistic and Borderline Disorders: An Integrated Developmental Approach*. New York: Brunner/Mazel, 1981.

Mayer, J. "The House of Bin Laden: A Family's and a Nation's Divided Loyalties." *New Yorker*, November 12, 2001.

McAllister, M. "Mohawks and Combat Boots: The Schizoid Dilemma of Punks." *Bulletin of the Menninger Clinic* 63, no. 1 (1999).

McBride, J. *War, Battering, and Other Sports: The Gulf between American Men and Women*. Atlantic Highlands, NJ: Humanities Press, 1995.

McDermott, T. *Perfect Soldiers: The Hijackers: Who They Were, Why They Did It*. New York: HarperCollins, 2005.

Menninger, Karl. *Man Against Himself*. New York: Harcourt, Brace, 1938.

Meyer, B.C. "Notes on Flying and Dying." *Psychoanalytic Quarterly* 52 (1983).

Middle East Media Research Institute (MEMRI). "Arab and Muslim Reaction to Terrorist Attack in Beslan, Russia." *www.memri.org*, no. 780, September 8, 2004.

———. "Former Kuwaiti Information Minister: 'Not a Single Fatwa Has Been Issued Calling for the Killing of Bin Laden.'" *www.memri.org*, no. 781, September 10, 2004.

———. "The Moderate Muslim Manifesto." *www.memri.org*, November 12, 2004.   frontpagemag.com/Articles/Printable.aspx?GUID=BF6692CF-225D-4675-9457-0E0A6470900E (accessed June 2, 2008).

———. "Osama Bin Laden Speech Offers Peace Treaty with Europe, Says Al-Qaeda Will Persist in Fighting the U.S." *www.memri.org*, no. 695, April 15, 2004.

Miller, J., M. Stone, and C. Mitchell. *The Cell: Inside the 9/11 Plot, and Why the FBI and CIA Failed to Stop It.* New York: Hyperion, 2003.

Momen, Moojan. *An Introduction to Shi'i Islam.* New Haven: Yale University Press, 1985.

Muñoz, J. "El Chico del círculo." *El Correo*, October 10, 2001.

Muqrin,`Abdul Aziz al-, *Saut al-Jihad* [The Voice of Jihad] 18, no. 3 (June 2004).

National Commission on Terrorist Attacks upon the United States. *9/11 Commission Report.* Washington, D.C.: Government Printing Office, 2004.

"19 Terrorists Obtained Social Security Cards." *Washington Post*, November 2, 2001.

Olsson, P. A. *Malignant Pied Pipers of Our Time: A Psychological Study of Destructive Cult Leaders from Rev. Jim Jones to Osama bin Laden.* Baltimore: PublishAmerica, 2005.

"Osama Says Taliban Rejected US Billions for Arrest." *Ausaf* (Pakistan), December 28, 1998.

Pape, Robert A. *Dying to Win: The Strategic Logic of Suicide Terrorism.* New York: Random House, 2005.

Patai, Raphael. *The Arab Mind.* New York: Hatherleigh Press, 2002.

Paz, Reuven. *Interview by Yoram Schweitzer*, September 19, 2004, Herzliya, Israel.

———. "Programmed Terrorists: An Analysis of the Letter Left behind by the September 11 Hijackers." International Institute for Counter-Terrorism (ICT), December 13, 2001.

Pentland, Alex (Sandy). *Honest Signals: How They Shape Our World*. With Tracy Heibeck. Cambridge, MA: The Bradford Book, MIT Press, 2008.

Peters, F. E. *The Children of Abraham: Judaism, Christianity, Islam*. Princeton, NJ: Princeton University Press, 2004.

Petersen, K. "The Pesantren at Surialaya." *Saudi Aramco World*, November–December 1990, 8–15. www.saudiaramcoworld.com/issue/199006/the. pesantren.at.surialaya.htm.

Pickthall, M. W. *The Life of the Prophet Muhammad: A Brief History*. Beltsville, MD: Amana, 1998.

Piven, Jerry S., Chris Boyd, and Henry W. Lawton. *Jihad and Sacred Vengeance*. Vol. 3 of *Psychological Undercurrents of History*. New York: Writers' Club Press, 2002.

Polish, Rabbi David. "Who Owns the Soul of Jerusalem?" *Reform Judaism Online*, June 2001, reformjudaismmag.net/601dp.html (accessed October 6, 2009).

Radlauer, D. "The Hijackings: A Pilot's View," September 13, 2001, www.nt-webweaver.com/flights.htm (accessed June 2, 2008).

Robertiello, R. C. "Physical Techniques with Schizoid Patients." *Journal of American Academy of Psychoanalysis* 2, no. 4 (1974).

Robins, Robert S., and Jerrold M. Post. *Political Paranoia: The Psychopolitics of Hatred*. New Haven, CT: Yale University Press, 1997.

Robinson, A. *Bin Laden: Behind the Mask of the Terrorist*. Edinburgh, UK: Mainstream Publishing, 2001.

Rose, Steven. *The 21st-Century Brain: Explaining, Mending and Manipulating the Mind*. London: Jonathan Cape, 2005.

Rotella, S. "Al Qaeda's Stealth Weapons." *Los Angeles Times* (September 20, 2003).

Ruthven, Malise. *A Fury for God: The Islamist Attack on America*. London: Granta Books, 2002.

———. *Islam: A Very Short Introduction*. New York: Oxford University Press, 2000.

Sabbah, F. *Woman in the Muslim Unconscious*. New York: Pergamon Press, 1984.

Sachs, S. "A Nation Challenged: The Videotape; bin Laden Images Mesmerize Muslims." *New York Times*, October 9, 2001.

Sawyer, F. *The Making of the Death Pilots*. Produced by J. Goetz, M. S. Singer, and C. Graeber. MSNBC Television, March 10, 2002.

Schmitt, Arno, and Jehoeda Sofer. *Sexuality and Eroticism among Males in Moslem Societies*. Binghamton, NY: Harrington Park Press, 1992.

Schurman-Kauflin, Deborah. *Disturbed: Terrorist Behavior Profiles*. Atlanta, GA: Violent Crimes Institute, 2008.

———. *The New Predator: Women Who Kill*. New York: Algora Publishing, 2000.

———. *Vulture: Profiling Sadistic Serial Killers*. Boca Raton, FL: Universal Publishers, 2005.

Schweitzer, Yoram. "Istishad as an Ideological and Practical Tool in the Hands of Al-Qaeda." *Journal of National Defense Studies* 6 (May 2008).

———. "We Love Death More Than You, Our Opponents, Love Life." Unpublished manuscript, 2009.

Schweitzer, Yoram, and Shaul Shai. *The Globalization of Terror: The Challenge of Al-Qaida and the Response of the International Community*. Edison, NJ: Transaction Press, 2003.

———. *An Expected Surprise: The September 11th Attack and Its Ramifications*. [In Hebrew.] Herzliya, Israel: Mifalot Publishing, the Interdisciplinary Center, 2002.

Segal, Hannah. "A Note on Schizoid Mechanisms Underlying Phobia Formation." *International Journal of Psychoanalysis* 35, no. 2 (1954).

Shoham, S. G. *God as the Shadow of Man: Myth and Creation*. New York: Peter Lang, 2000.

Simons, M. "What's in a Name? For a Saudi Insider, Everything." *New York Times*, February 7, 2004.

Sina, A. "The Force Behind Muhammad." *FaithFreedom.org* (n.d.). www.faithfreedom.org/Articles/sina/10306.htm (accessed June 2, 2008).

Slackman, M. "Many in Jordan See Old Enemy in Attack: Israel." *New York Times*, November 12, 2005.

Souchard, P. A. "French Authorities Arrest Two Suspects in Connection with Terror Investigations." Associated Press, June 5, 2003.

Spencer, R. *Islam Unveiled: Disturbing Questions about the World's Fastest-Growing Faith.* San Francisco: Encounter Books, 2005.

Stein, Howard. "The Scope of Psycho-Geography: The Psychoanalytic Study of Spatial Representation." *Journal of Psychoanalytic Anthropology* 7, no. 1 (1984).

Tauber, E. S. "Symbiosis, Narcissism, Necrophilia: A Disordered Affect in the Obsessional Character." *Journal of the American Academy of Psychoanalysis* 9, no. 1 (1981).

Timimi, Sami. *Pathological Child Psychiatry and the Medicalization of Childhood.* New York: Routledge, 2002.

Trifkovic, Serge. *The Sword of the Prophet: Islam: History, Theology, Impact on the World.* Boston: Regina Orthodox Press, 2002.

Turki, Thuraya Al-, and Huda Zuraik. "The Change of Values in the Arab Family." *The Arab Future*, October 11, 1995. Quoted in "Honor Killing," 2002.

Ullman, Richard B., and Doris Brothers. *The Shattered Self: A Psychoanalytic Study of Trauma.* Hillsdale, NJ: Analytic Press, 1988.

Vaknin, Sam. *Malignant Self Love: Narcissism Revisited.* Edited by Lidija Rangelovska. Prague: Narcissus Publications, 2003.

Victor, Barbara. *Army of Roses: Inside the World of Palestinian Women Suicide Bombers.* Emmaus, PA: Rodale, 2003.

Volkan, Vamik D. *The Need to Have Enemies and Allies: From Clinical Practice to International Relationships.* Northvale, NJ: Jason Aronson, 1988.

Volkan, Vamik D., and R. T. Corney. "Some Considerations of Satellite States and Satellite Dreams." *British Journal of Medical Psychology* 41 (1968).

Von Kellenbach, Katharina. "A Pilgrimage to Belarus." *Aish.com*, October 30, 2004, www.aish.com/jewishissues/jewishsociety/A_Pilgrimage_to_Belarus.asp (accessed June 2, 2008).

Waldman, P. "A Historian's Take on Islam Steers U.S. in Terrorism Fight." *Wall Street Journal*, February 2004.

Wangh, M. "The 'Evocation of a Proxy.'" *Psychoanalytic Study of the Child* 7 (1962).

Weaver, M. A. "The Real bin Laden." *New Yorker*, January 24, 2000.

The Week. March 26, 2004.

Wehr, Hans. *Arabic-English Dictionary: The Hans Wehr Dictionary of Modern Written Arabic.* Edited by J. M. Cowan. Ithaca, NY: Spoken Language Services, 1976.

Westermarck, Edward. *Ritual and Belief in Morocco.* 2 vols. London: Macmillan, 1926.

Wilgoren, J. "After the Attacks: The Hijackers: A Terrorist Profile Emerges that Confounds the Experts." *New York Times*, September 15, 2001. query. nytimes.com/gst/fullpage.html?res=9C0DE1D61F38F936A2575AC0A 9679C8 (accessed June 2, 2008).

Wolff, E. C. "Flying: Psychoanalytic Observations and Considerations." *Psychoanalytic Study of the Child* 37 (1982).

Wright, Lawrence. "The Terror Web." *New Yorker*, August 2004.

Wright, R. "Since 2001, a Dramatic Increase in Suicide Bombing." *Washington Post*, April 18, 2008, www.washingtonpost.com/wp-dyn/content/ article/2008/04/17/AR2008041703595.html (accessed April 18, 2001).

Wrye, H. K. "Projections of Domestic Violence and Erotic Terror on the Film Screen." *Psychoanalytic Review* 84, no. 5 (1997).

Zeidan, Ahmed. *Bin Laden Unmasked: Meetings Whose Publication Were Prohibited by the Taliban.* Beirut: The World Book Company, 2003.

INDEX

ABOUT THE AUTHOR

Nancy Hartevelt Kobrin is a counterterrorism specialist and a psycho-analyst. An expert on posttraumatic stress disorder (PTSD), Kobrin contribut-ed to the section on short-term psychodynamic therapy in *Effective Treatments for PTSD* (Guilford Press, 2000). She has presented at the North Atlantic Treaty Organization; has given seminars to police and military intelligence agencies in Israel, Spain, and Sri Lanka; and has taught U.S. Army military intelligence courses in Missouri and Florida. She is currently in training as a social scien-tist in the Human Terrain System program at Fort Leavenworth, Kansas, and is set to deploy to Afghanistan. She earned her PhD in Romance and Semitic languages and semiotics, and she is currently studying Dari and some Pashto.